BRIGHT.BAZAAR'S
DREAM DECOR

BRIGHT.BAZAAR'S

DREAM DECOR

STYLING A COOL, CREATIVE AND
COMFORTABLE HOME, WHEREVER YOU LIVE

WILL TAYLOR

jacqui
small

For Toby

First published in 2016 by
Jacqui Small LLP
An imprint of Aurum Press
74–77 White Lion Street
London N1 9PF

Publisher: Jacqui Small
Commissioning and Project Editor: Joanna Copestick
Managing Editor: Emma Heyworth-Dunn
Senior Designer: Rachel Cross
Art direction and Styling: Will Taylor
Location Research: Will Taylor
Illustrations: Serena Olivieri
Production: Maeve Healy

ISBN: 978 1 910254 28 8

A catalogue record for this book is available from
the British Library.

2018 2017 2016
10 9 8 7 6 5 4 3 2 1

Printed in China

Quarto is the authority on a wide range of topics.
Quarto educates, entertains and enriches the lives of
our readers – enthusiasts and lovers of hands-on living.
www.QuartoKnows.com

CONTENTS

BRINGING DREAM DECOR HOME

To me a well decorated home is a collection of personal dividends gathered from one's own experiences of and adventures in travel or day-to-day personal surroundings. I've lost count of the number of times a new-to-me place or seeing a routine experience in a new light has resulted in an overwhelming urge to bottle up one of these many sensory feelings to bring back home and into my decor. I'm often at my happiest by the ocean with salty, windswept hair, barefoot, with sand between my toes; nothing to crowd my mind beyond the endless roll call of blue hues. I often use these dreamy experiences and blue pool tones to inform the decor of my own interior space.

REFRESH & REVIVE
In Will Taylor's London home office, blue and yellow shades referenced from a statement gallery wall combine to create a balanced palette that offers a refreshing and reviving vibe for an inspiring workspace.

A TOUCH OF SUNSHINE

What does your dream decor look like? The answer to this question is undeniably different for each and everyone of us. Sure, there will be similar decorating elements and themes that may appeal across the board, but ultimately your home is unique. That's the exciting reality of decorating: you have the opportunity to create a completely personal space that reflects your distinctive character and taste.

When I am working on an interior design scheme for my home I always try to bring a touch of sunshine to each room. Yellow and blue are my favourite colours, so I weave these hues into most spaces in my apartment. In some spaces I pair the hues together, as seen in the palette of my home office which was inspired by the colours I saw in a small fishing village in the Indian Ocean. The energizing qualities of the weathered yellow wood on the boat were tempered perfectly by the soothing array of blue hues – it was the ideal colour combination to encourage productive work in my home office, and so it became the natural focus of the decorative scheme.

In other schemes I like to use yellow sparingly as an accent hue, or blue as my key primary colour and then layer in other colours such as a splash of hot pink, as an accent instead. For example, in my open-plan living and dining room I use sunshine yellow and dusty pink as accent colours to inject hue into the monochromatic base palette. I hung two pieces of abstract art above the white linen sofa as a point of reference for my chosen accent

DESK ACCESSORIES
A hand-painted striped vase filled with yellow roses complements a blue ceramic vessel holding a scented candle and a graphic notebook that sit upon the desk in this London home office (above).

INSPIRATION STATION
On the Indian Ocean island of Mauritius a weathered yellow painted wooden boat and the surrounding blue hues of the ocean (opposite top) were the catalyst for the colour palette in Will Taylor's office (opposite below).

ARTFULLY ACCENTED
Crisp white walls and sheer linen curtains maximize the natural light that floods into Will Taylor's London home office. The simple white palette allows for an oversized photographic art print of Central Park, alongside a mix of blue and yellow decorative accessories to layer well in the space (opposite below).

TWO TO TANGO

A white linen sofa provides a neutral base to layer on typographic and patterned cushions in this London living room. Pattern is also introduced via a glass lamp base and statement abstract artworks (above).

DOT TO DOT

Scandinavian-designed ink-splattered wallpaper sets the tone for this Scandi-meets mid-century dining nook in Will Taylor's London home. Marble and metallic touches soften the industrial iron bookcase, while a circular yellow artwork echoes the pattern in the wallpaper behind (opposite).

colours. The black and white scheme used as a basis for the room allow some freedom to reference different colours from the statement artwork on the wall. I can then layer these colour accents into the room on cushions, vases and decorative accessories. I love this approach to decorating my home because it keeps the schemes flexible enough to quickly switch up the colour dial, by swapping in smaller, transitional pieces in new accent colours. It's important to remember that there's no right or wrong when it comes to how your home should look. In this book I don't wish to tell you how your home should be, but rather share my hints, tips and decor know-how that I hope will make dream decorating easier and more enjoyable for you.

Perhaps you have a rough idea of the sorts of dream decor looks you like but you are struggling to pin down the right mix for you ? Or maybe you are set on a look but need some pointers on how to break it down into the individual decorating elements to recreate it in your current space? Or do you simply just love peeking inside inspiring homes of all shapes and sizes (I'm right there with you!). It's for all of these reasons that I decided to write my second book on the topic of dream decor. I'm keen to show that no matter where you live you can create a cool, creative and comfortable space to call your own. I've started the book by walking through some key decorating elements that are central to almost every interior design scheme. Learning how to use these in your decorating arsenal will be a great asset as you begin to create your own dream decor. And there are eleven unique decor styles waiting to inspire you. Happy decorating!

Will Taylor

TICKLED PINK

Serene blues are punctuated with splashes of hot pink accents in this colourful yet soothing bedroom scheme. Japanese artworks are referenced across the bedding and upholstered headboard. The wooden bedside table, inspired by a 1940s sideboard found at a Parisian flea market, adds character and charm.

Keep the fundamental elements of a room white if you wish to mix and match colours and patterns.

SCANDI MIX

The living room in Will Taylor's London apartment includes flashes of pattern and accent colour that add visual interest to a classic monochromatic scheme. A jet-black feature wall enlarges the space, while neutral furniture allows for mix-and-match cushions to be introduced.

Understanding the key elements of decor will give you the confidence to mix up the ingredients of a room to create a stylish space that's personal to you.

DREAM ELEMENTS

Breaking a room's decor down into key elements can really help to simplify the process of decorating. My philosophy is that there are six key elements to consider when it comes to creating a new interior design scheme: colour, pattern, texture, furniture, lighting and accessories. A food recipe is much easier to follow when you have all the ingredients prepped and ready; the same is true of designing a room. Understanding how – and when – to use these six elements will lay the foundations for a sensational room.

BROWNSTONE CHARM
A pair of grand chandeliers lends an opulent vibe to the classic exposed brick walls of Benjamin and William's brownstone property in Harlem, New York City. A vintage rug, matadors and an elegant iron bed complete the scheme (opposite).

DREAM ELEMENTS

As you read this chapter you will see how the elements of a room begin to build, eventually all joining forces to create the final scheme. Trust me when I say we've all experienced that overwhelming feeling when you face a blank space or a challenging room that needs a makeover. These are the projects where I find it useful to split the decorating process out into segments. It not only helps you to plan the project and the necessary steps involved, but also makes it easier to be aware of the more minute details and decisions that you will need to consider at each stage.

When you start planning a decorating project it always helps to break up the requirements of the space and the project, then consider the design direction for each individual element. This approach will help you to manage and plan your decorating scheme, but it's important to make sure you don't consider any one of the room's elements in a vacuum. Yes, tackle one element at a time, but do reflect on your plans for said elements in unison with the other pieces of the scheme. This method of decorating will help you create a more cohesive and professional-looking space.

When Kristina Lindhe found a piece of vintage blue-and-white-striped fabric she knew it would be a perfect item to frame for the wall of the living room in her family home (opposite). Knowing that this would be the focal point of the space allowed her to layer in other elements within the room with confidence. The blue and white pieces of furniture, accessories and lighting all echo the hero piece and create a coordinated yet soothing living space.

THE WHITE WAY
The all-white palette in this Swedish living room gives a zen-like base to layer in colour, pattern and texture via an array of fresh greenery, textiles and wooden furniture. The stripes of the artwork and cushions are a subtle introduction of pattern in the space.

BACK TO BLACK

Metallic brass touches soften the all-black cabinetry in this kitchen in Manhattan Beach, California. A tiled splashback introduces pattern, while the white and brass pendant fitting brings depth to the overall scheme.

PATTERN ON PATTERN

Will Taylor clashes patterns to create visual interest in the living room of his London home. A solid striped rug is accented with a green tree motif tray, while a bunch of white peonies references the key monochrome palette.

COLOUR

Your decorating toolbox is nothing without colour: it's one of the most influential elements in any decorative scheme. Whether you like to go all out with hue or keep things pared back with occasional accent splashes, introducing colour into your rooms will pay you plenty of design dividends. Over the coming pages I'll show you how to use colour to make design statements; how to layer it into a space sparingly via accessories; and share my insights on how you can discover the colours you love to make choosing hues simpler. Ready, steady, colour!

AWASH WITH HUE
Wood panelling has been lavished with a generous lick of racing green paint to give the bathroom of this Hamptons property a colourful yet serene vibe (opposite).

COLOUR INSPIRATION

When it comes to figuring out the colours you love the easiest thing to do is to take a long look around you. Quite simply, take in everything you see as you go about your day. Of course it can be great to get inspiration while on holiday, but equally you can discover new hue ideas by taking a moment to look at your everyday experiences in a new light – walking a different route to work; eating lunch in the park instead of at your desk; or looking at the packaging you like while shopping in the grocery store, for example.

As a self-confessed colour addict I like to document many of my day-to-day colour inspirations on Instagram via the #MakeYouSmileStyle hashtag. There are now thousands of Instagrammers posting their own day-to-day colour inspirations and discoveries on the hashtag – why not take a look for instant access to a bank of shades from all corners of the world? I find it a wonderful and instant way to get inspired if my creative juices are feeling jaded.

When you start to pull your colour inspiration together – tear sheets, holiday photographs, Instagrams, swatches and so on – see if you can notice any commonalities in each piece. When I visited Miami, Florida for the first time I found myself drawn to all the incredible blue hues of the locale. From painted wooden furniture and ceramic bowls in a restaurant to the intense natural shades of the ocean, I could easily see which colour inspired me most.

MIAMI VIBES
The ombre ocean colours seen from Miami Beach (opposite above) were the catalyst for a colour inspiration story during a trip to Florida. Hand-painted blue tableware and a hanging blue-painted wooden swing (opposite below) also gave me ideas for decorating with blue back at home. Photography is a great way of capturing colours you love so you can refer back to them when planning a new interior design scheme.

Occasional splashes of hue in otherwise neutral spaces are all that's needed to make a stylish colour statement.

SPANISH SPLASH
Eero Saarinen Tulip chairs upholstered in raspberry fabric jolt vibrancy into this dining room on the Spanish Balearic Island of Menorca. Hand-thrown ceramics and fresh blooms create a relaxed, exotic atmosphere (above).

RURAL & RUSTIC
Painted window trims in green lend a gently colourful vibe to Martin Bourne's kitchen in Upstate New York. Freestanding storage and a metal Belfast sink complete the pastoral country look (opposite).

BALANCING COLOUR

Living comfortably with brighter colours is artfully demonstrated in the Upstate New York home of Martin Bourne. A prop stylist by trade, Martin has layered a series of bright hues across the otherwise neutral palette of his country home. He has managed to create a gently colourful scheme in the living room by balancing his brights with calmer, neutral shades. The key elements of the space that take up the largest surface areas – the furniture, walls and floors – are all introduced into the space in neutralizing grey and browns. This gives the room the breathing space that's required to carry the peppering of brighter elements that Martin layered into the scheme to add vibrancy. The colourful elements are all anchored to a multi-hued rug under the sofa and coffee table. From there, a duo of colour-blocked cushions jolt life into the solid couch, while an eye-catching blue artwork draws the eye back through the room. By surrounding these brighter hues with a neutral base palette and a series of idiosyncratic art, the scheme feels balanced, personal and comfortable.

COUNTRY QUIRK
A talented prop stylist brings an offbeat touch to the art that decorates the walls of their country home in America. A tufted neutral ottoman is accessorised with flea-market finds, while splashes of colourful accents break the grey-brown palette.

STATEMENTS

If you are looking to make colour the central decor element of your scheme you can choose two main routes. The first is to create an all-over colour statement, such as wallpaper or paint across all walls. Alternatively, you can introduce a lone splash that stands out in a neutral space. You can achieve this look via a vibrant bedspread draped over white bedding, or an oversized piece of art hung in a pared-back living room.

The dining room (opposite) in the Hollywood Hills home of Jesse Tyler Ferguson and his husband Justin Mikita sees all four walls adorned with opulent studded midnight-blue wallpaper. This creates a cocooning, cosy and dramatic atmosphere

that sets the perfect tone for entertaining. The couple took the opposite approach to making a colour statement in one of the guest bedrooms (below). Here a blue anchor motif and bed sheet add a striking and graphic colour focal point into the otherwise neutral, textural scheme.

COLOUR CLUB
A dark wood panelled ceiling, midnight-blue wallpaper, brass wall scones and a statement glass pendant create a gentleman's club atmosphere in this Los Angeles home (opposite).

BEDROOM BUOY
A calming nautical ambience is present in this Hollywood bedroom thanks to a reclaimed wooden bed and anchor motif bedding (below).

DIVINE DARKS

The black feature wall in this Manhattan Beach living room creates a dramatic statement that anchors all the elements of this predominantly monochrome space. From the rug to the artworks, everything in the room links to the wall, to create cohesion.

ACCESSORIZE WITH COLOUR

Embellishing a room with colourful accessories works well if you layer in shades from the main colour palette or introduce new accent colours. The former works well in a tonal or monochromatic scheme where there is a single colour in the palette. For example, this living room (left) shows how a series of black and white accessories – a graphic tree-print cushion, a polka-dot vase and delicately patterned curtains – all echo the black wall behind. An alternative approach is to introduce a new colour into the scheme via colourful accessories. The dining space in this Brooklyn warehouse apartment (right) shows how a punchy red lampshade and seat cushion pair with opulent metallic finish vases to brighten the white painted brick walls. Accent colours are typically only 10% of a space, and by layering them in sparingly the result is often dramatic.

SCANDI INFLUENCE
Sophisticated monochrome palettes seen in many Scandinavian homes inspired the palette of Will Taylor's living room in London. Pattern is introduced via accessories and textiles to add interest to the black walls (left).

COLOURFULLY COOL
A vintage sideboard and chair are dressed with flea-market finds to create a colourful vignette in this Brooklyn apartment. Meanwhile vibrant red colour accents bring a bright vibe to the cool white walls.

PATTERN

Pattern and colour often go hand in hand, so it helps to consider the two decorating elements in tandem when planning a scheme. Much like colour, pattern is a great decorating element for creating a design statement, so it's important to get the balance right. In this section I'll show you where to look for pattern ideas as well as share inspiring and unique ways in which you can invite the patterns you love into your home. Do you like to mix, match and clash everything from shapes, and dots to simple lines? Perhaps a pared-back approach to pattern is your style? Either way, read on to get inspired by both looks.

PICK 'N' MIX PATTERN
Jesse Tyler Ferguson and Justin Mikita's Hollywood Hill's master bedroom shows how clashing patterns, from a striking chevron chest of drawers to bold check bedding, can result in a style statement. Keeping the patterns within one colour family ties the whole look together (opposite).

PATTERN INSPIRATION

Seeking out pattern inspiration for a new decor scheme can feel overwhelming at first, but stick with it, because much like Hugh Grant's famous line in the movie *Love Actually*, pattern, actually, is all around us! I often stumble across inspiration for pattern when I least expect it. The key to discovering pattern you are drawn to, is to consciously take note when you pause to do a double take. Perhaps it's when you walk into a restaurant and notice the geometric tiles underfoot, or maybe it's the fabric on the inside of your favourite shoes? The possibilities of pattern are endless.

One of the things I find helpful when cataloguing my pattern inspirations is to note how often the combination of the colours used and the design of a pattern combine to inspire me. This means I can narrow down both the hues and graphic elements of a new scheme in one go. Remember to keep a visual note of everything from city wall art and statement tiles to fabrics and grocery displays for original pattern ideas.

Introducing pattern into a room can pay both design and personal dividends for a long time. I often use pattern to remind me of experiences I've enjoyed. The tree print pattern in my living room (page 34) for instance, was inspired by the memory of a snowy walk through a forest in Norway.

SEEKING PATTERN
I seek out pattern ideas during my day-to-day activities and document these on Instagram. During a hotel stay in the Hamptons the stripes on stripes (opposite above left) of my espadrilles and the carpet showed how layering pattern can create a striking statement. The arrangement of fresh berries (opposite above right) at a Stockholm market inspired me to use block colours in thirds, while the wall art of multi-coloured repeat circles (opposite below left) by The Most Famous Artist at The Springs in Downtown Los Angeles also caught my eye. Tiles are one of my regular sources of pattern ideas, such as these blue and white shapes (opposite below right) I saw in an entryway in London.

GEOMETRICS

Geometrics are a sure-fire way to add personality to a space. Originally they were popular during the 1960s 'Mod' period but have enjoyed a resurgence in popularity in recent times. Whether you opt for elementary patterns like dots, squares or triangles, or more complex designs of diamonds, hexagons or octagons, geometrics will add a graphic punch to your scheme. A headboard upholstered in chevron fabric, a Greek key rug laid under the coffee table or wallpapering the alcoves either side of a fireplace in a diamond design are just a handful of stylish ways to introduce geometrics into a scheme.

Tiles offer a perfect opportunity to add a geometric touch to a room. In the kitchen you could create a cool coffee shop vibe with small hexagonal tiles underfoot, or why not create a chic spa vibe in a bathroom with floor-to-ceiling hexagonal tiling? This will create a focal point in itself and lends an understated glamour to a wall.

HEX-MEX
Hexagonal tiles and a cool white marble sink surround lend a sophisticated and calming atmosphere to the bathroom of this historical Yaletown loft in Vancouver. Industrial cage pendant lights give the overall scheme a subtle masculine edge (above left).

HEX LUXE
In their Harlem brownstone home, Benjamin and William laid a hexagonal tiled floor that, paired with brass pulls and hardware, creates an opulent yet cool aesthetic in the kitchen (below left).

COLOUR AS PATTERN

Pattern is best friends with colour. Using both of these decorating elements in sync can lead to an effortlessly stylish-looking scheme. The reason these two elements work so harmoniously is because they each have the power to tame or enhance the visual strength of one another in a scheme. For example, if you wish to heighten the visual power of a striped cushion on a sofa, opting for a multi-coloured stripe design will create more of an eye-catching statement than a design that uses a single hue. Equally, a delicate floral pattern can reduce the zing of a colour block wall in any living space.

A pattern-on-pattern approach, such as using floral on stripes, is an example of how to accessorize with two textiles in the same palette. This technique brings depth to the striped design while softening the overall scheme by introducing pattern in a floral form, providing another layer of interest.

LAYERING
Kristina and Tommy Lindhe paired graphic stripes and delicate florals to create a stylish red scheme in the entryway of their Swedish home. All-white walls and painted wooden furniture allow the pattern and colour to shine (above right).

TEXTILE BRIGHTS
A statement cushion splashes vibrant colours and lines into the living room of this Hollywood home. A soft and subtle chevron pattern on the blue throw extends the pattern theme in the space (below right).

PATTERN MIX

The Willow pattern wallpaper and a tufted indigo headboard give this Miami bedroom a classic, sophisticated vibe. The glass-sphere pendant and simple black-stripe curtains then inject a modern twist.

PLAYFUL PATTERNS

An ink-splatter cushion, painterly abstract artwork and an ombré ceramic tray introduce a relaxed atmosphere into this London living room. A classic black-and-white striped mid-century lamp and and checked throw keep the scheme from feeling juvenile.

STRIPES

One of the most enduring patterns used in decor terms is the humble stripe. Its classic look feels right at home in living spaces across a wide spectrum of styles, from traditional to contemporary. The reason the stripe is so popular is its ability to visually alter the feeling of space in a room. The small corner in this Swedish bedroom (opposite) is an example of how wide vertically-striped wallpaper can add height to a small space. The thick stripes give the illusion of space by drawing the eye upwards and into the space above the chair. In a Hamptons home (left) a thinner ticking stripe is used to add subtle detail to a sand-coloured armchair. In this design a thick stripe would detract from the shape and form of the chair itself. When decorating with a bold stripe it's best to keep pattern to a minimum in other key elements of the space, such as on furniture, so that the eye has a natural focal point.

SUBTLE STRIPE
Proving that stripes don't have to be graphic or headline-grabbing, the thin ticking stripe of the armchair in this American Hamptons home is subtle and stylish (left).

BOLD & BLUE
Kristina and Tommy Lindhe wallpapered a spare bedroom in their Stockholm house with thick blue and white stripes to give the illusion of more space. A battered leather armchair and striped rug lend a comfortable and cosy vibe to the room (opposite).

NAUTICAL DREAMS

An ocean-inspired palette
brings a serene atmosphere
to this London bedroom. The
midnight-navy upholstered
headboard provides a
backdrop to simple white
linen bedding and a striped
bedspread, while a hot pink
sheet nods to the accent
colour in the Japanese prints
above the bed.

DECORATING WITH FLORALS AND FLOWERS

Whether you choose to introduce real flowers or floral patterns and prints into your dream room, they both help to bring the essence of the outdoors into your home. There is a multitude of fresh ways to introduce a floral print into a room: assemble a collection of vintage floral plates mounted as a wall display above a dining table; have your favourite floral print fabric stretched and framed above the couch; place a large-scale floral rug under the sofa and coffee table or use a bold floral tablecloth in an otherwise neutral-coloured kitchen. The possibilities are numerous. The key to getting florals right in a space is to consider whether the room would benefit from a delicate, detailed floral print or a large-scale floral pattern. The former is ideal for small introductions of floral pattern, such as an accent throw cushion or vase. The latter works best on bigger 'statement' elements of a scheme, such as an oversized canvas artwork or area rug.

If you opt to bring a large-scale floral into a scheme, be sure to consider its impact upon the other elements in a room. Notice how Martin Bourne placed a sofa upholstered in a solid fabric (opposite) in front of some statement floral artwork in his Brooklyn apartment – this provides a welcome visual break from the large pattern and also serves to lend more emphasis to both the sofa and the wallpaper individually. Alternatively, a quick way to add an instant focal point to an empty nook is via a vase of freshly cut blooms placed in a tall vase.

DELICATE BLOOMS
A tall, textured vase is filled with freshly cut white blooms in this upstate New York kitchen. The contrast between the rough vase and the delicate flowers results in an attractive visual tension in this vignette (left).

METALLIC PRINT
An unexpected metallic finish to the canvas in Martin Bourne's Dumbo, Brooklyn apartment breathes life into a traditional floral pattern. A mid-century sofa and colourful accessories round out the look (opposite).

LIVING WITH FLORALS

Florals are a decorating element that feature strongly in the dream decor line-up for many people, but sometimes can be intimidating to use. By following a few simple guidelines, you'll be on the right track to creating a space that feels fresh and floral. Remember that the scale of a floral will change how it looks: a big print on a small item, such as a cushion, looks modern and graphic; a small scale floral on the same item creates a vintage, shabby chic feel. In Martin Bourne's upstate New York living room, he uses a large-scale floral print via half-height wallpaper on the walls. By choosing a white floral print against an aged-green background hue, the resulting look is passive enough to allow for additional prints in the space. Martin added these elements via a gallery wall of artwork hung in front of the floral wallpaper. He has introduced a small-scale floral painting as a nod to the countryside locale of the house, but keeps a modern edge to the overall scheme by pairing it with abstract pieces of modern art. A helpful hint is to remember that when decorating with florals it's all about the details. For example, if you wish to have an upholstered sofa, avoid a skirted bottom if you want a contemporary look, as this will instantly make the print look antiquated.

MIX IT UP
The living room of this American country house includes florals in the form of both large and small-scale prints. Pairing them with a tufted grey couch, glass antique coffee table and contemporary art lends a trad-meets-mod look.

TEXTURE

Dream homes are those packed with heart and soul. And I believe the soul of a space often lies in its texture. Living in a space is about how it makes one feel – the tactility of a room is one of the key sensory experiences that make a successful space. As such, this decorating element is an essential part of any scheme. Some spaces lead with texture as their hero – such as a kitchen with rough exposed wooden cabinetry – while others see this decor element introduced sparingly, through a pile of worn vintage suitcases, for example. In this chapter I'll show you how to decorate around texture from structural elements, like an exposed brick wall, through to introducing texture via new pieces.

HAMPTONS BOUND
A pile of old suitcases and a bamboo director's chair bring texture to the corner of the master bedroom in this Hamptons home. The wool rug lends additional tactility underfoot, too (opposite).

TEXTURE
INSPIRATION

Sometimes when I find myself taking a photograph of a scene that inspires me I have an overwhelming urge to reach out and touch the contents of the frame. It's at this point I usually signal the 'texture inspiration' alert in my brain. I find that this inspiration comes about in one of two ways: firstly through sight – seeing and feeling the urge to experience the tactility of a surface – and secondly through the unexpected feeling of a texture; when walking barefoot, for example, or touching weathered wood. Great texture adds detail and depth into a space, and you know when texture has worked in a room because it's almost as if you can feel it, without physically touching it.

When I arrived at this bar in Miami (opposite below) I was far more excited by the textures at play in the decor than the cocktails I could indulge in. My eye was drawn to the trio of rattan pendant shades; their sand-like hue was perfect for the beach surroundings. Underneath them was a line-up of mix-and-match blue and white wooden stools. Each stool's weathered finish meant that it took on an individual patina and texture. It was these textural elements that instantly told the decor story of the bar: casual, sensual and exotic.

TACTILE TIMES
Repetition and texture took centre stage in the decor of this Miami bar (opposite below) thanks to three rattan pendants and a series of blue and white rustic wooden stools. The wall-mounted woven trays (opposite above left) in the lobby of a hotel on the island of Mauritius create a striking textural statement, as does this wall covered in reclaimed colourful wooden shutters sourced from old Mauritian homes (opposite above right).

COUNTRY CHARM

The all-white kitchen of this renovated schoolhouse in Pittsburgh, PA tells a charming texture story; wooden beams painted milky white pair with white subway tiles, factory pendants and cabinetry to create a light, cool and calm environment. The open wooden shelving and island unit lend a comfortable and informal feel.

The corner of this dining room in a renovated Pennsylvanian house demonstrates how to mix up finishes and surfaces to tell a texture story. From the rustic wooden wine rack to the metallic lamp and tea set, each element of the decor hangs together with an easy and natural cohesion.

HOW TO BRING TEXTURE HOME

By appealing so strongly to our senses, texture adds dimension to a room. It's this that makes it an important decorating element. Layering and varying the surfaces and finishes of a decorating scheme is what makes for an intriguing and memorable space. Sometimes texture can be added through an understated jute rug underfoot, for example, or more overtly through a rustic wooden dining table. When you are choosing the finishes, furniture, and accessories for your room consider how you can use each piece to add a textural element into the space. Take these three spaces as examples: the weathered wooden wine rack in a Pittsburgh home adds visual texture, whereas the linen bedding in a New York City apartment injects tactile texture to temper the rough visual texture of the exposed brick walls. Thirdly, ceramics and a bowl of fresh lemons upon a paint-splattered, untreated wooden dining equal a rustic scheme.

SOFT TOUCH
The rough visual texture of exposed brick walls mixes well with a chandelier to add romance and mirrors to bounce natural light into the space (below left).

COUNTRY CONTRAST
Smooth hand-thrown ceramics are effortlessly juxtaposed with a bare wood table in a home on the Spanish Balearic Islands (below right).

BLACK MAGIC
High gloss black subway tile lines the walls of a Harlem brownstone bathroom, while metal wall lights and an industrial wooden storage table bring about a subtle nautical vibe.

TOUGH LUXE
The contrast of delicate glass in a brass pendant light with the mirrored bedside table and an exposed brick wall creates perfect levels of design tension in the master bedroom of this New York City home.

VINTAGE VIBE

Prop stylist Martin Bourne invites texture into his apartment in Dumbo, Brooklyn, NY through a mix of vintage storage units and flea-market finds such as fans and mirrors; painted brick walls, wooden cladding, taxidermy, succulents and fabric drapes round out the eclectic look.

FURNITURE AND LIGHTING

I like to think of furniture as the 'bones' of a space and lighting as the nerve centre and also the costume jewellery. The analogy I find helpful is: just as a body is dressed in an outfit, you dress a space with furniture and lighting. In both examples you start with the body or space, dressing the former with the clothes and the latter with furniture, before accessorizing both with finishing touches. The importance of choosing the right clothes for the right body is also true when it comes to home decor: picking the right furniture and lighting for a space is key to the success of an interior, with lighting providing atmosphere and warmth.

ARTFULLY COLLECTED
A Moroccan coffee table and metallic pouf, a Hans Wegner Papa Bear wingback chair and a vintage wooden sideboard result in an eclectic yet cohesive set of furniture in this Brooklyn, New York City warehouse apartment.

FURNITURE INSPIRATION

It's the times when I am out of my own home that I find myself inspired by different furniture styles. Whether I'm in a bar, restaurant or hotel room, it's in these moments that I try to take in the aesthetic of the space in order to reflect upon my own furniture edit, and how I might be able to switch up my personal mix the next time I come to refurnish or decorate. A memorable moment of furniture admiration came to me when meeting friends for drinks at Schiller's Liquor bar on Manhattan's Lower East Side (opposite left). The restaurant and bar were furnished with cool industrial designs, from weathered metal Tolix chairs and mix-and-match cafe tables to iron-strip lighting and fans. As my furniture purchases often reference Scandinavian and mid-century influences, I was pleasantly surprised by how drawn I felt to the more industrial forms and styles within the space and how happily they sit alongside a mix of accessories ranging from Art Deco mirrors to period-piece tables and graphic floors.

My New York visit left me with a renewed sense of awareness for how I choose my furniture, and it made me realize how opening my eyes to new styles and furniture eras was a catalyst to evolving my personal style back at home. The coming pages are full of ideas and inspiration that I hope will do the same for you, providing visual pointers that allow you to 'see' new possibilities when out and about, finding furniture and lighting you can layer into your dream home.

INDUSTRIAL EDIT
The furniture selection in these New York City bar/restaurants, Schillers (opposite left) and Upland NYC (opposite right) created an industrial and layered look that felt cohesive yet casually unstructured.

WAREHOUSE STYLE

A Parisian homeowner creates an unexpected industrial look to her open-plan Paris apartment via a custom-built iron staircase, exposed brick walls and a large factory pendant. A generous loose linen sofa and Eames rocker give a stylish yet welcoming feel amongst the harder elements of the scheme.

CREATING DREAM SPACES

As the 'bones' of any room, furniture is the central decorating element that will help you to create spaces for practical, comfortable and stylish living. After all, it's the physical pieces you invite into a room – the chairs, tables, lamps, coffee tables and so on – which set the tone of the space and indicate its lifestyle function – from relaxing to working or, perhaps, a mix of both. Spaces for relaxing are decorated with indulgent, deep sofas, whereas rooms for working take on a more functional vibe via tables with large surface areas and straight-backed chairs for support.

Jesse Tyler Ferguson and Justin Mikita used furniture to mix up the pace of their property across a variety of spaces, each of which are decorated to have different functions in their Hollywood Hills home. As the couple already have a chic dining room (page 31) for entertaining, they were keen to have a more casual breakfast area. School chairs and a window seat around an oak table are used to create this vibe in a light-filled nook of their kitchen. Meanwhile, their cinema room takes on a clubhouse vibe with low-slung armchairs, a tapered leg coffee table and wall pendants with exposed filament bulbs. Keep a look out at flea markets and vintage stores for one-off furniture pieces such as vintage side tables or mid-century chairs and tables then combine them with industrial light fittings for a comfortable but stylish vibe.

CASUAL DINING

A brass ceiling pendant draws the eye down and creates a cosy and casual dining area in this Los Angeles home. A pair of owl cushions lends a playful note to the space (above).

ROOM TO VIEW

The cinema room of this Hollywood home is multi-purpose thanks to a series of vintage armchairs placed around a wooden coffee table. A hideaway screen can disappear when the room is required for reading only (opposite).

ACCESSORIZING FURNITURE

With the bones of your scheme in place you can begin to focus on the accessorizing elements that will give the room those all-important finishing touches. You build a decorating scheme by making choices about colour palette, patterns, textures, lighting and furniture, and in doing so you will have been writing the story of the space. Although a room, in my book, is always evolving, it's the accessories that are the final chapter to write when creating a scheme. This is convenient, because it is by considering, then implementing, all the previous decorating elements in this chapter that you are likely to have created a scheme in which layering-in accessories will be a breeze. You can switch them out to create a new look or vibe as your taste or a change in season dictates.

The patio design of this Miami apartment plays with graphic pattern and rich colours to create a striking design story. Pieces of Delft pottery are placed proudly on wall-mounted plinths to create an eye-catching statement feature, while the play on repetition ties in with the graphic stripes of the rug. With strong pattern underfoot and a statement wall feature, it works to keep the main pieces of furniture relatively simple, with deep navy upholstery accessories and a peppering of cushions in accent colours to reflect the natural environment.

In New York, a couple adorned their simple wall-mounted shelving unit with a series of copper pans and kitchen accessories that speak to their love of cooking and entertaining. Think of accessories as the decorating flourishes that will help you stamp your mark on a room.

CULINARY ACCOMPANIMENTS
A textured brick wall is brought to life with an array of copper pans and colourful enamelware in a display range across a chunky industrial-style metal shelving unit (above).

MIAMI VIBES
Pops of colour and pattern are layered into the patio space of this modern Miami apartment via a series of colourful cushions and eye-catching Delft pottery (opposite).

STORAGE IDEAS

No room is complete without practical storage, especially in spaces where there's a healthy arsenal of necessary equipment to house, such as a kitchen. Although practicality is key in such spaces it doesn't mean you need to let go of style. This kitchen shows how building storage solutions into the heart – i.e. bones – of the space can pay dividends on design and practicality. This welcoming space (opposite) sees a pair of weathered iron lockers placed back-to-back in the centre of the kitchen to create an instant island unit. Not only does this provide bountiful storage, but also it offers a solution for food preparation, entertaining and creates an interesting focal point in the room.

Meanwhile generous floor-to-ceiling storage options are fully explored via wall-mounted cabinetry, bespoke cupboards and under-table shelving. Eye-level cabinets make it easy to access items but also allow the kitchen to retain a spacious feeling throughout.

LOCKER ROOM

Introducing repurposed locker units personalizes this New York kitchen and provides masses of storage in the centre of the space (left).

MODERN ELEGANCE

Luxurious marble countertops and brass fixtures and fittings sit alongside white subway tiling and sophisticated grey cabinetry to create a space that oozes modern style (below).

DISPLAY

The fun part of creating your dream decor is putting the pieces you love on display. The personal items, finds gathered from travels, treasured pieces of art or heirlooms passed down from loved ones in generations gone by, these make up the fabric of our lives and are perfect for displaying in our homes. If you think of furniture as the bones of the room, then think of the accessories and pieces you display there as the elements that dress those bones.

When it comes to creating a display, think about the look you are aiming to achieve. If your dream display equals a visual that is graphic, clean-lined and symmetrical, then a series of equally-sized art is an easy way to achieve the look. However, if you'd rather a more eclectic look that displays a variety of items then opt for a looser approach to how you display the collection: mixing up the sizes, textures and materials to give a gathered vibe.

Assemble your display directly on the wall, on display shelves or a tabletop for impact.

TRIO TRICK
A series of three artworks by the same Japanese artist hung alongside one another create an instant graphic statement in this London bedroom (below).

COLLECTED MEMORIES
Wooden panelling is adorned with gathered finds, taxidermy, a vintage fan and photographs personal to the owner of this Dumbo warehouse apartment in Brooklyn, NY.

LIGHTING

A common misconception about lighting is that it should be decided right at the end of a decorating project. I believe lighting is a key element in the bones of a space and should be considered from the moment you begin to plan a new decorative scheme. Thinking about how you will light the space you are creating from the outset will impact upon your furniture choices too. For example, if you plan on having a large overarching floor lamp that hangs over the middle of the room, you may wish to opt for a low-sitting couch and coffee table, along with flush ceiling light fittings, in order to maximize on visual space in the room. Similarly, a lighting statement created, for example, through repetition of the same pendant three times, would mean that it would not work to introduce matching armchairs or a triptych of artworks, as this would distract from the impact created by the trio of pendants.

The large hanging glass hurricane lamps in this Hamptons, New York home are a fine example of how knowing your lighting solutions from the start allows you to decorate accordingly to create a considered space. Here the soft white curtains, French iron day bed dressed in neutral textiles and vintage storage barrel are quietly sophisticated touches that support the overall look of the space yet still allow the hurricane lamp to occupy the spotlight.

Lighting is a great decorating element to use to your advantage when looking to create a visual design statement, especially in an empty nook. The reclaimed ship pendant (below) ties in perfectly with the nautical theme of this Hamptons home, and its striking nature turns an unmemorable corner into a conversation starter in the space.

SEA STYLE
A reclaimed ship searchlight makes a striking feature in a quiet corner in this coastal home on New York's Long Island. A life ring and a vintage nautical tin complete the maritime vibe (below).

COOL & CALM
Chris O' Shea and her wife Ashby created a refined and stylish look in their Bridgehampton, NY house. A romantic iron day bed maximizes natural light from the large windows dressed in long white curtains. Vintage finds take the place of coffee and side tables, while a hurricane lamp is the statement piece in the space (opposite).

Repetition is an easy way to introduce a striking design statement into a room. For an informal look, opt for odd numbers; for a more structured feel, go even.

PERFECTLY PLACED
A hanging 'halo' of exposed lightbulbs sunk into a metal circle creates both impact and a soft light in this Spanish-inspired Hollywood Hills living room (above).

CENTRE POINT
The owners of this renovated schoolhouse in Pittsburgh, PA suspended an oversized industrial-style metal factory pendant above a reclaimed dining table. Mesh dining chairs echo the material of the light fitting and help create a cohesive scheme (right).

BRINGING IT ALL TOGETHER

As I close out this chapter on decorating elements I am keen to show an exemplary space that pulls all six of the decorating fundamentals – colour, pattern, texture, furniture, lighting and accessories – together in a seamless and effortless fashion.

This Miami living room is a stylish example of how to bring all the decorating elements together and make them work. Here we can see how a statement gallery wall of art is used as a jumping off point to layer in colour, pattern and texture across furniture, lighting and accessories that all refer back to the art in some way. The rattan blind recalls the texture introduced via the bamboo frame hung on the wall; the intense blue hues in the main artwork are continued across the sofa and dining chairs; the graphic striped prints are repeated in the curtains hung across the ceiling-to-floor glass window. The smart use of each decorating element across everything in the room is what creates a synergized and stylish scheme.

My hope is that this chapter will have prepped your decorating toolkit, built on your knowledge of fundamental decorating elements and inspired you to create a space that equals your dream decor.

MIAMI ELEGANCE
Considered use and repetition of each decorating element means the varying colours, patterns and textures of this Miami living room combine to create an elegant and multi-layered space.

DREAM STYLES

Italian rustic or Brooklyn industrial, Parisian chic or Scandi cool. Whatever your interior aesthetic, I believe that your vision of dream decor needn't be a daydream for the future – it can be a reality now. While it's common to aspire to, say, a larger bedroom or to have more storage in the kitchen, you can still create a space to love where you are right now. That's why I was so keen to write this book: I'm passionate about people being able to create homes that they love to be in, where they are proud to invite loved ones to visit and where they are excited to come back to, no matter how good their holidays may have been!

CLASSIC COASTAL
Maritime finds lend a cool coastal vibe to this neutral-led palette in the Hamptons, NY. A rattan chest and lampshade invite texture into the space (opposite).

DREAM STYLES

The following eleven homes all differ in style, but the common theme between them is a cool, creative and comfortable approach to design that can be emulated no matter where you live. In the mix you will see how industrial and cool casual styles harmonize unexpectedly in a small Paris apartment; how classic country style is given an injection of urban personality in a renovated schoolhouse; why a Spanish Colonial Hollywood hills works with a gentleman's club twist; how a rustic Spanish home plays with colour and texture to stunning effect; and how a tiny NYC apartment can ooze charm and practicality – alongside many more inspiring interior design takeaways.

You may find a single look you love from floor to ceiling – hurrah! But remember you also have the freedom to play mixologist with the decor styles. Pick and choose components from each style to create a line-up of decorating elements that equate to your dream space. Try not to let the physicality of your current home deter you. So you love the tall iron cabinet from Industrial Loft but lack space? Introduce the look via a small side table, or a lamp instead. Or maybe you long for an all-white floor in the living room but are unable to make such a major change. Easy: invest in a large-scale area rug instead. A savvy approach to a decorating project will lead to dream schemes.

To show how I seek design inspiration, each style chapter begins with my travel photographs – these are my main source of ideas for decorating schemes. A recipe notebook then shows how to translate the inspiration into an interior scheme. This is followed by an in-depth look at the individual decorating elements of each style to demonstrate how each homeowner created their interior. I hope this will inspire and lead you to discover the decorating elements that you'd like to invite home in order to create your dream decor.

COLOUR SPLASH
A hero blue sofa leads the colour story in this London living room. Bright art is grouped to create a striking gallery that adds interest to the crisp white walls.

MEDITERRANEAN MARVEL

inspired by Santorini, Greece

Santorini was unlike any other Greek island I've ever stayed on – yes, the traditional Greek blue colour adorned countless churches, weathered shutters and doors as expected, but nothing could have prepared me for the abundance of texture and incredible island views. Santorini is almost horseshoe-shaped because of a caldera (caused by the mouth of a volcano collapsing to create a crater of water). As such, you can look back at other parts of the island from almost anywhere. The topography of the dark volcanic island alone is striking, but against the intense mass of a still-as-a-millpond dark blue sea, a sky so clear it could be glass and sun-soaked cave houses tumbling down the side of the cliffs, the juxtaposition of all these elements at once is absolutely captivating. It's this seductive Greek spirit that sits at the heart of the Mediterranean Marvel style.

THE CONTRAST OF COOL, CRISP WHITE AGAINST THE AZURE BLUE OF THE SKY, OCEAN AND WEATHERED SHUTTERS SITS AT THE HEART OF MEDITERRANEAN DECOR. BY EXPLORING THE ROAD LESS TRAVELLED TO SMALLER, QUIETER CORNERS OF THE ISLAND OF SANTORINI, MY MEMORIES WERE STRONGLY STIRRED UPON MY RETURN HOME. TUCKED AWAY AT THE FOOT OF THE NORTHERNMOST TIP OF THE ISLAND, AMOUDI BAY IS FRAMED BY WHITEWASHED BUILDINGS AND BOUGAINVILLEA. IT FELT LIKE A TRUE IDYLL.

ΑΓΡΟΤΙΚΑ - ΠΡΟΙΟΝΤΑ
ΚΡΑΣΙ - WINE
ΦΑΒΑ - FAVA
ΒΙΣΑΝΤΟ - VISANO
ΝΤΟΜΑΤΑΚΙΑ - TOMATOS
MELI - HONEY
ΣΤΑΦΥΛΙΑ - GRAPE
ΤΣΙΠΟΥΡΟ - TSIPURO

RECIPE FOR MEDITERRANEAN STYLE

WEATHERED WOOD · BURST OF YELLOW · EARTHENWARE · WHITE-WASHED WALLS · BLUE AND WHITE · PAINTED SHUTTERS · AZURE SKY · TERRACOTTA · SUNSHINE ACCESSORIES · COOL LINENS

Translating the seductive colours and textures of Greece into your home is simple: take your lead from the classic colour contrasts. Sit vivid shades of azure blue against fresh whites and accent the palette with shots of hot pink inspired by the abundance of bougainvillea. With your palette set, turn to the textures found in many traditional Greek buildings to direct your material choices. Create textural interest in the space by juxtaposing rough stone walls with cool tiled floors and soft linen upholstery. A peppering of organic elements – a bowl of citrus fruits and vase of cut blooms, for example – are the perfect finishing touch. I was particularly inspired by the sun shimmering over gently lapping crystal-clear blue waters and the vivid hues visible as the fishermen returned in colourful boats with their fresh catches. It inspired me to embrace the allure of the island's intensely exotic blue hues once I was back at home.

Blue and white is one of my absolute favourite colour combinations and nowhere is it more crisp and vital than in the jewel-bright setting between the Mediterranean and the Aegean sea. Combining these shades in varying degrees of intensity, area and texture is often a winner, whatever shade of blue you choose as your keynote.

Once you've worked out whether you wish to have white or blue as your base, you can then think about layering in furniture, fabric or accessories in complementary tones or textures to punctuate the space.

VIVID CONTRAST

Take your cue from the bright colour contrasts that occur organically in the Mediterranean by injecting pockets of hot pink or sunshine yellow into an otherwise two-tone blue and white space (above left). Introduce these into a home via vivid tiles in a bathroom (above right, top) or via painted wooden furniture (above right, bottom).

EXOTIC ECCENTRIC

A stylish line-up of quirky painted portraits, handmade ceramics, flagstone flooring, a reclaimed, paint-splattered dining table and a series of Saarinen-designed Tulip chairs combine to create the Mediterranean Marvel style in this dining room. The unassuming white wooden beams and ceiling pair with stone tiles underfoot to create a neutral canvas. It's onto this pared-back base palette that the colourful personality of the homeowner, Spanish shoe designer Ursula Mascaro, is reflected. Eclectic and exotic, yet refreshingly approachable, the marriage of vibrant colour and tactile texture as the scheme's lead elements make a striking space.

EASY BREEZY

The dining room of this Menorcan home is a lesson in effortless layering, where rough wooden texture marries seamlessly with tactile linens and smooth Saarinen chairs.

ISLAND LIFE

The lure of the coast is undeniable but whether you live on a small island just moments away from the sea, or in an inner-city apartment, there are several decorating elements you can use from your toolkit to bring home the laid-back vibe that's central to Mediterranean island style.

Ursula Mascaro decorated her Spanish Balearic Island home with a seemingly effortless touch that reflects the slow pace of life on the island. The utilitarian concrete floor that runs through several of the downstairs rooms is painted azure blue. This makes a statement feature out of an existing element of the space, and although cooling in nature, here the blue adds subtle warmth and a strong colour to the otherwise white painted stone walls.

Curated treasures that reflect the island are peppered throughout Ursula's home. Small touches such as coral, earthenware, hand-thrown ceramics and vintage finds lend a creative and casual vibe to her space. Look out for such individual items on your travels: pieces that remind you of your visit but work well in a relaxed scheme back at home.

FEELING BLUE
A blue painted concrete floor blue in this Spanish home instils colour and personality to the space (top right). Texture is introduced via an iron sideboard and stone walls, while collected treasures and handmade pottery add visual interest to a cool white scheme (bottom right).

BLURRED LINES
A large patio door helps to blur the line between indoor and outdoor living, while a pair of wooden deckchairs encourage lazy afternoons in the sunshine (opposite).

FOUR STEPS TO
DIVINE ISLAND STYLE

01: HANDMADE CERAMICS When it comes to perfecting that effortless island style, you need to focus on simple, beautiful accessories that tell an exotic story of their own. Tactile handmade vases, platters and bowls, some with a lick of painterly blue watercolour, will evoke the ocean.

02: BOLD HUE Using a hit of strong, vibrant colour is a great way to nod to the indulgence of hedonistic and laid-back island living. Here, the painted azure blue floor serves as an anchor to vintage finds, such as found paintings and wicker screens, all layered against a crisp and cool white backdrop. The stark contrast between the blue and the white is softened by the introduction of textiles and soft furnishings.

Play with contrast to keep the Mediterranean Marvel style fresh – an unexpected splash of colour will inject life into an otherwise pared-back palette.

03: LAYERED TEXTURE In this neutral take on the exotic style, textural elements are used front and centre to create a relaxing yet visually interesting and tactile space. When using textures as the lead element of a space it's important to achieve balance. Here we see how soft linen seat pads soften the cool white brick, while the faded hues of a Kilim rug are tempered further by terracotta pots, a smooth wooden table and battered vintage poufs.

04: INDOOR–OUTDOOR VIBE Extending the home to create an indoor-feel outdoors is central to the Mediterranean Marvel style. The key is to maintain a laid-back relaxed vibe via mix-and-match neutral pieces of furniture, potted succulents and a low-lying entertaining table for filling with aperitif nibbles at the golden hour.

BALEARIC BEAUTY
This open-plan living
and dining space has a
seamless quality thanks to
layers of colour and texture
on a white backdrop.

HEDONISTIC HIPSTER

inspired by Brooklyn, New York

Thanks to the borough of Brooklyn, New York has arguably become known as the home of the hipster. From the moment I stepped out of the subway to stroll through Williamsburg, the hedonistic vibe of the district was apparent. Given the flurry of bicyclists, I could have been forgiven for thinking I'd been transported from Manhattan to Amsterdam. I sidestepped around coffee shops and bars that had spilled out onto the pavement, their weathered mix-and-match colourful cafe chairs accompanied by pumping music. Vintage furniture stores popped up sporadically down little side streets, and converted warehouses with lashings of natural light and factory windows were dotted on almost every corner. The lifestyle appeared carefree and indulgent, yet despite the laissez-fare approach of the area, it always felt coordinated and stylish too. In fact, it was the area's confident personality and original flavour that made me fall for Hedonistic style in a big way.

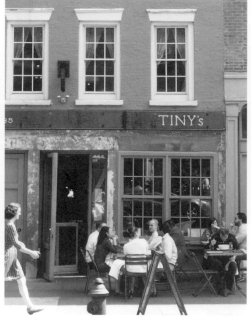

BROOKLYN'S MIX OF TRADITIONAL BROWNSTONE
BUILDINGS AND HISTORIC NEIGHBOURHOODS INSPIRED
THE REFINED URBAN LOOK OF THE HEDONISTIC HIPSTER
DECOR STYLE.

RECIPE FOR HEDONISTIC HIPSTER

VINTAGE PAINTINGS · RECLAIMED WOOD · WHITE PAINTED BRICK WALLS · FLEA-MARKET FINDS · BOTANICAL TOUCHES · COPPER KITCHENWARE · BRASS · MID-CENTURY FURNITURE · SUBWAY TILES

The Hedonistic Hipster style is a fusion of influences from across Manhattan and Brooklyn in New York. It takes inspiration for its decorating elements from the sleek midtown Manhattan structures and marries them with rougher elements triggered by the more historic areas of Downtown New York and Brooklyn. Subway tiles reflect the smooth and elongated panes of skyscraper glass, while bare brick walls are a nod to the cobbled streets and old-age charm of the city's older districts.

The key words for this decor style are: rustic, reclaimed and refined. The look is about balancing textural leads in the space, such as reclaimed wooden cladding and exposed brick walls, with smooth and sophisticated marble tabletops and white subway tiles. Amongst these two elements, reclaimed furniture, art and accessories found at flea markets should be introduced to give the look a timeless appeal. The colour palette should reflect the muted tones of Brooklyn brownstones, with occasional flashes of hue introduced through blooms or vases. Group old paintings together and hang above a mid-century-inspired marble sideboard to create a space that successfully fuses old with new decorating elements. This decor style is fluid and ever-changing; displays evolve as you find new treasures. It's a look that works best when reclaimed materials and items of subtle colour combine in an effortless cohesion. The best way to achieve this is to follow your instinct and introduce quirky pieces you love into a space.

RECLAIMED TOUCHES

White-washed exposed bricks or reclaimed wood make for a textural addition to an interior (above left). Old, battered signage and wooden tables will continue the rough notes of the space. Create a subtle heritage feel with a buttoned leather headboard (above right) or connote a cool, hipster feel with polished brass wall lights (above right, top).

RUSTIC & RECLAIMED STYLE

For a look with lasting intrigue and interest, the Hedonistic Hipster style is your best friend. Created by blending subtle Scandinavian sensibilities (bleached wood floors) with chic Brooklyn elements (oversized subway tiles) and curated flea-market finds, this layered look brings warmth, rustic charm and easygoing city chic in spades. This ever-evolving approach to decorating is demonstrated with ease via the Lower East Side home of props stylist Anthony D'Argenzio in New York City. Paintings sourced from Anthony's travels across the globe adorn the walls, while mid-century inspired furniture sets a retro tone for his gathered space.

ROUGH & READY

A bleached wood floor and white painted exposed brickwork brings a fusion of rough and smooth textures to this light-filled Lower East Side apartment in Manhattan.

BOHEMIAN BOTANICALS

The Hedonistic Hipster style embraces greenery and uses it as a decorating element to soften the rougher textures of the look, and enhance the laidback vibe of the interior. Here in Anthony's NYC apartment we see how he strategically places a variety of botanicals, such as a Banana Leaf plant, as a way to mix up the textures on display throughout his home. Softening the strong lines of the mid-century-inspired designs, these green touches also help to vary the height and colours at play in the space, which brings depth into the scheme in the process. Hang small succulents from existing features – a door handle or wall light – to encourage an organic look.

FLEA FINDS
A collection of vintage paintings offsets the cool white brick of the wall behind (opposite), while a mid-century-inspired marble sideboard is softened with a colourful vignette of paintings and flea-market finds (above) . A houseplant provides some natural relief suspended in a planter from a brass wall fitting.

HEDONISTIC HIPSTER DECOR CUES
FOR MAXIMUM SMALL SPACE STYLE

01: SHOW IT OFF Forget minimalism! A small space doesn't mean you have to hide everything away. Instead, think of shelving units as mini stages on which to store and display your favourite wares. By repurposing reclaimed wooden planks as open kitchen shelving, the homeowner of this small NYC apartment has not only utilized the surfaces available for storage, but also created a layered, character-packed space filled with memory-sparking pieces.

02: CLEVER COMPACT A folding table that doubles as a sideboard means a dining table in a small open-plan space can still look like it's part of the room even when it's not in use. By treating the middle section that is always left 'up' as a sideboard, with styled accessories and blooms, it helps the piece to blend into the rest of the space.

03: BUILD IT UP When space is at a premium, make the most of the surface area of your walls by utilizing the whole area for storage and display. Installing built-in, wall-mounted storage units in the same colour as the walls will blend the storage into the room. Here the refreshing qualities of white maximize the light and airy feel: a matt, milky shade on the walls blends seamlessly with the white storage unit.

04: PLAY WITH CONTRAST Create visual depth in a small space by contrasting dark with light. Here a gallery wall of vintage framed ship blueprints and photographs stretches along the white panelled walls of the apartment's narrow hallway, helping to elongate the space.

CREATING A CASUAL CAFE-STYLE KITCHEN

Anthony and his wife opted for sleek, oversized white subway tiles to help elongate the snug space available in their narrow corner kitchen. A casual cafe vibe is encouraged via open shelving created from reclaimed wooden planks. The contrast between the bright white and dark, rustic wooden counter and shelving not only provides depth but prevents the scheme from feeling too cold or sterile. Avoiding wall-mounted cabinetry is a smart design move when it comes to a small kitchen: not only does it give the impression of added space, but it gives the kitchen a welcoming, homely feel.

OPEN FOR BUSINESS
The owner of this NYC apartment took inspiration from bar design by hanging glasses from hooks, ensuring they utilized the top and bottom of the shelves (above right). Displaying your wares makes it quick and easy to reach what you need when cooking (above left), while hanging cafe pendants, bar stools and brass cooking pans create a relaxed vibe in this small kitchen.

Cladding flat walls with rustic wood panelling will add texture into a room that lacks original features.

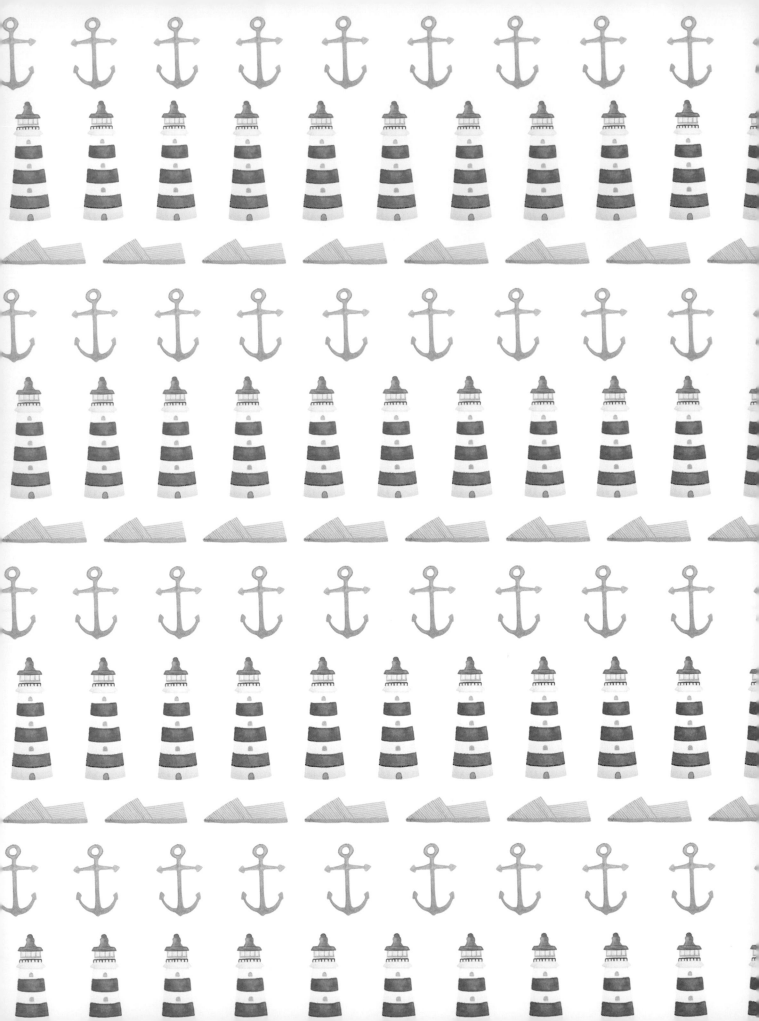

COASTAL RETREAT

inspired by The Hamptons, NY

The lure of the coast is ever present for me. Not only do I feel at my most relaxed when I'm near the ocean, but I also gain an abundance of inspiration for my decorating schemes. In fact, the natural elements of the coast, and the maritime details that pepper coastlines around the world, offer ideas and inspiration for some of the most timeless decorating elements. One of my favourite coastal towns is Sag Harbor, a small village in the Hamptons. Whenever I take a trip there I am inspired to invite home everything that I see and feel. And this spark of inspiration is true for many. From the rough wooden textures of the harbour jetty and classic shingle cottages, to the boundless neutral shades of the beach and blues of the sea, the natural environment is a guide for numerous possibilities regarding the texture, colour and pattern of decorating elements that make up nautical schemes, whether or not they are located by the water. This chapter details how to make a coastal retreat of your own, wherever you live.

ROUGH WOODEN TEXTURES AND FISHERMEN'S FLOATS
CREATE A NATURALLY NAUTICAL VIBE IN THE
HAMPTONS. FOR A PERFECT COASTAL RETREAT,
A STRONG DEVOTION TO SIMPLICITY IS KEY.
AIM FOR A PALETTE THAT ECHOES THE SEA,
THE SAND AND NATURAL MATERIALS
FOR A TRULY RELAXING ATMOSPHERE.

RECIPE FOR COASTAL RETREAT

JUTE RUGS · NAUTICAL STRIPES · COOL GREY WALLS · CERAMIC TILES · WOODEN FLOORS · WEATHERED FURNITURE · GRAIN SACK LINEN UPHOLSTERY · GRAPHIC MOTIF TEXTILES · ROPE

The natural patterns, textures and colours I saw in Sag Harbor in the Hamptons, NY are the ideal catalyst for coastal decorating elements. Walking along the beach and seeing the eclectic mix of pebbles inspired me to think about neutral decorating palettes.

For a more sophisticated take on the strictly maritime navy and white colour scheme, experiment with pale but warming grey and cream hues against wooden and painted furniture.

One way of getting a coastal scheme to look cool and not twee is to use classic maritime elements and graphics sparingly. While a coastal space isn't complete without an anchor cushion or worn wooden oar, a mere peppering of these elements may be all that is required to tell the coastal story. Surround these ubiquitous nautical decor pieces with a palette inspired by the natural elements: painted wooden furniture in a weathered finished, cool grey painted walls, linen upholstery and thick, tactile and comfortable jute rugs underfoot. Fill sofas with cushions to up the comfort factor – this dream decor is all about escaping and relaxing, after all. Soften cool schemes by inviting the coastal outdoors in, with vases of blue and white blooms, and employ some graphic nautical motifs across soft furnishings and accessories to provide visual interest. Keep floors simple; wooden floorboards work best for a coastal atmosphere.

NAUTICAL NOTES

The most stylish way to create a dream coastal retreat with a maritime feel is to layer subtle elements that reference the coast. Rope storage bags and white tongue-and-groove panelling (above top, left and right) spell out seaside style. Neutral textiles (above left) are a nod to the natural coastline; while jute baskets layered on to crisp white create a fresh feel (above right).

COASTAL COMFORT

Photographer Chris O'Shea and her wife Ashby Dodge called upon their shared love of vintage pieces, Chris's Dutch heritage and classic nautical design elements to create an effortlessly comfortable coastal home in Bridgehampton, New York. The fusion of their gathered pieces in the main living space is anchored via the calming grey painted walls and a series of striped elements introduced across an occasional armchair, rug and textiles. Rope covered glass lamps, anchor motifs and fresh hydrangeas bring home the dream decor elements inspired by the nearby ocean to create their coastal retreat.

NEUTRAL DIRECTION
The living room of this Hamptons, NY home marries calming neutrals, from a jute rug and vintage sand linen upholstery, to a simple white sofa to create a coastal look.

LIVING WITH WHITE

Whether milky-cool or paper crisp, decorating with white offers a multitude of design options whatever your desired look. Here, the kitchen in Chris and Ashby's Bridgehampton, New York home shows how living with white is anything but plain. The fresh white walls and flooring of this coastal retreat are broken up by geometric white tiling, which provides a graphic, textural backdrop to the rest of the kitchen elements. A trio of iron pendants, marble countertops and a wooden island unit create a striking contrast against the layered whites.

WHITE & BRIGHT

This Hamptons kitchen is proof that white on white works. Pattern and texture are used to add visual interest through a ceramic splashback. Found blue glassware filled with rope, and vases filled with fresh Hydrangeas stylishly nod to the coastal surroundings, gently offsetting the white base palette.

NAUTICAL TOUCHES

Whether you live by the coast or not you can call upon classic nautical design elements to bring home a coastal look. Organic elements such as driftwood and shells inject the texture of the ocean into a space. Meanwhile, graphic elements like anchors, brightly painted oars and reclaimed porthole windows instantly recall images of relaxing days by the sea. A peppering of these elements in each room is enough to tell the design story; foil them with a gentle neutral background colour to keep the look feeling fresh.

DESIGN DETAILS

This coastal American home has been accessorized with a series of nautical pieces, from anchor objects and prints (above left, top and bottom) to reclaimed vintage pieces such as a weathered wooden seafood restaurant sign (above right). The home's stairwell (opposite) is adorned with a large life-ring and a painted wooden rowing oar doubles up as a handrail.

SHUTTER SURPRISE

A beautiful reclaimed blue-painted wooden shutter has been placed on stone plinths and repurposed as a dining table in this Bridgehampton, NY home (this page). A vintage ship searchlight and found items such as wooden oars and food storage tins are collected together to decorate a small corner (opposite).

FOUR WAYS TO ACE
NAUTICAL STYLE

01: COOL COLOURS The colours of a coastal scheme work best when kept within a mostly neutral palette. When introducing stronger colours – reds, greens and yellows, for example – do so via faded, cool shades from the colour family. Here soft apple green walls pair with a light yellow throw and pillows with flashes of muted raspberry.

02: STATEMENT PATTERN Introducing pattern in unexpected ways can help to make a design statement out of an existing feature in a space. In this Hamptons home the fronts of each step on the staircase have been papered with a striking Greek key-like effect that catches the eye.

03: CLASSIC MOTIFS Inject the feeling of the ocean onto a plain white sofa via characteristic elements that are typical of the coast. A linen cushion embellished with a large blue anchor image instantly tells the maritime design story, while a blue and white star and stripe blanket echoes the timeless palette of this look.

04: WEATHERED TEXTURES Texture plays an important role in coastal decor. In this Bridgehampton space a distressed wooden cabinet in blue is the ideal home for a collection of ceramics. Linen drapes soften the rough elements of the space, while a brass bell and wall light add further layers of interest.

To allow for the layered elements of a coastal scheme keep your main palette a simple white or grey.

SITTING COMFORTABLY

An antique French daybed and a duo of hanging hurricane lamps are the hero elements of this light-filled living space. The rest of the living room in this Hamptons home is accessorized with soft neutrals – sheer white curtains, stone and white cushions and a repeat pattern rug.

CURIOUS COLLECTOR

inspired by the Brooklyn Flea

With every visit to the Brooklyn Flea I am left inspired by a new discovery. In the warmer months the flea market is set right on the water in the borough's hip Williamsburg neighbourhood, and in the shadow of the impressive Manhattan skyline across the East River. The market itself is littered with stalls, each offering an eclectic mix of vintage furniture or artisans selling handmade pieces. If I visit with no goal or particular piece in mind it's always fun to see what my haul looks like. The Flea is equally worth a visit for dedicated collectors; whether it's old clocks or costume jewellery, Eames chairs or Delft pottery, one can always find a treasure to add to a collection. The home of the Curious Collector is far from minimalist and never trite – this chapter shows how to emulate the enigmatic look at home.

SEEING A MISCELLANEOUS MIX OF VINTAGE ITEMS — CAMERAS, FOOD TINS, GLASSWARE, FANS, LICENSE PLATES — INSPIRED ME TO CONSIDER A GATHERED 'COLLECTED' DECOR STYLE. THE BROOKLYN FLEA, WHERE I FIRST FOUND SUCH A GREAT COLLECTION OF DECORATING PROPS, IS JUST ONE OF MANY INSPIRING FLEA MARKETS AROUND THE WORLD, FROM PARIS AND LONDON TO PASADENA, LA, MADRID AND MUNICH.

RECIPE FOR
CURIOUS COLLECTOR

VINTAGE FANS · HERITAGE TINS · COLOUR BLOCKING · GLOBAL FINDS · FURNITURE CLASSICS · OVERSIZED PAINTINGS · CURATED DISPLAYS · CERAMICS · OLD CAMERAS · MIX & MATCH RUGS & HIDES

Goodbye minimalism! When it comes to building a Curious Collector scheme the best approach is to mix up the recipe of decorating elements as per your own treasured finds. That's the great thing about curating a collected look at home: you are quite literally decorating your space with collections of things that you love. Whether it's old vintage cameras sourced from flea markets, or a set of glassware handed down through your family for generations, it's these personal displays in the decorating scheme you design that will tell the curious story of your home.

To stop a collected space looking cluttered or messy, arrange items of a similar nature in groups upon coffee tables, sideboards and on the walls. Use the collections to help zone open-plan spaces or tell an interesting decor story in a single vignette. In a quiet, empty corner you can create a successful focal point in this way. Also, use bold blocks of colour and pattern that will serve as an anchor behind, say, a series of vintage jewellery and photography grouped together on a wall or a panel of vintage signage, to provide a visual focal point in the space. Give the overall look an air of class by introducing one or two furniture classics, such as a Hans Wegner Papa Bear wingback armchair, a mid-century modern Bertoia chair or a statement light, whether a Best light table lamp or a floorstanding focal point like the coveted Arco floor lamp by Castiglioni.

THE ART OF CURATION

Pulling together your finds and favourite things into displays and collected groups is a quick and stylish way to create great displays. A gallery wall may serve as a frame for industrial lockers (above right) or fill the walls of a bathroom (above left, top). Alternatively, a classic Bertoia chair found at a flea market could offset a copper bathtub (above left, bottom).

CURIOUSLY CURATED

Professional props stylist Martin Bourne brings his natural flair for styling an eclectic mix of items from his job into his warehouse apartment in Brooklyn's Dumbo neighbourhood. A large vividly coloured surfboard is casually propped up in one corner, and it's this piece that sets the tone for the diverse design edit throughout the space. A vintage sofa, metallic leather pouf and a series of painted portraits combine to create a colourful, personality-packed home.

QUIET ECHO

The subtle repetition in the design choices of this New York City loft and the assorted mix of furniture, lighting and accessories still feels cohesive. This is achieved via matching tables, a pair of occasional chairs and light metallic finishes that echo across art and furniture.

MIXING COLOURS

As with the varied contents of his home, Martin also mixes an array of hues across the decor of his open-plan warehouse space. Wooden panelling painted in a light apple green shade provides a cool backdrop for layered shades from brighter colour families. An intricately patterned Moroccan coffee table introduces a number of colours to the space, one of which – a raspberry red – is echoed via the upholstery of a Hans Wegner Papa Bear wingback chair. Meanwhile a vintage wooden sideboard is treated like a stage and used as a platform for a vignette of colourful art, quirky objects and books.

PLAYFUL PERSONALITY
A plain olive green sofa (above) is accessorized with gathered finds from frequent trips made to New York City and upstate flea markets by the owner of this Dumbo apartment. A metallic floral print stretched over a large canvas brings vivid pattern into the room, while painted portraits break up the pattern. Elsewhere in the space, a collection of vintage chairs, sideboards and tables grouped together in the main living room set an interesting retro vibe (opposite).

FOUR WAYS TO
LIVE WITH COLLECTED TREASURES

01: BEDROOM BLISS Exposed brick white walls, plain bedding and a simple white chest of drawers allow the bed, walls and surfaces of this Dumbo, NY warehouse bedroom to be dressed in flea market finds. A casually propped ladder is an opportunity to drape the next day's outfit, while the white bedding allows for statement pillows and a bright blue vintage map bedspread.

02: VIBRANT VIGNETTE Treat coffee tables like stages and use them to display your much loved treasures and finds. The key to making a vignette a success is to vary the heights, textures and colours within the display to create an interesting visual. Here a tall, skinny vase placed upon a pile of books pairs perfectly with a piece of coral flocked in electric blue.

03: LET LOOSE Don't be afraid to let your collections run wild. Take the desk space of this Brooklyn home as inspiration where an unstructured display of stationery, postcards, jewellery, ceramics and photographs group together to give a creative, arty vibe. The vintage fan adds structure and form to the display.

04: CAPTURE COLOUR Use colour as a backdrop to help group and frame your collections. In the open-plan dining room of this Dumbo apartment in New York City a lick of green paint provides a colour block to anchor a series of collections in the space, from vintage vases and cups to artworks and books.

EXPANSIVE VISION
Martin Bourne's eye for detail and colour brings a cohesive feel to the gathered and layered approach he takes to decorating his open-plan warehouse home in Brooklyn, New York's Dumbo neighbourhood.

COLOURFUL COUNTRY

via Burano Island, Italy

Unlike Venice where the canals are lined with terracotta and neutral shades, Burano – a small island 40 minutes away by boat – contains row upon row of rainbow facades. The individual hue of each home and building lends the island masses of character From a distance the buildings look like storybook sets; up close, their weathered paint texture and age-old street names juxtapose neatly with an abundance of cheerful colour. Alongside the colour, I also found another classic country decorating element: tiny stores all over the island selling lace. 'Nonnas', often wives of fishermen, sat on stone steps or old wooden chairs, deep in conversation as the colourful lace they had made billowed in the wind around them. The fishermen are the reason why the houses are each painted a different colour. They left to fish early and returned late so the bright colours helped them locate home. It's this bold approach to hue that inspired colourful country.

THE CONFIDENT USE OF COLOUR ON
BURANO ISLAND, ITALY, ENCOURAGED ME
TO EXPLORE HOW BOLD HUES CAN
INJECT LIFE INTO COUNTRY DECORATING
SCHEMES. AT TIMES IT'S THE UNLIKELY
JUXTAPOSITIONS OF COLOUR THAT
WORK IN THESE BOLD COMBINATIONS.
SOMETIMES BLUE AND GREEN CAN BE
SEEN, FOR INSTANCE; EQUALLY, CANARY
YELLOW PUNCTUATED WITH RED CAN
ALSO WORK IN RELATIVELY SMALL DOSES.

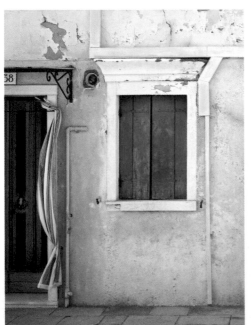

RECIPE FOR
COLOURFUL COUNTRY

PATTERNED TILES • PAINTED WINDOW FRAMES • MIX AND MATCH CHAIRS • COLOURFUL FINDS • STAINED WOOD FLOORING • ACCENT COLOURS • MOROCCAN BOUCHEROUITE RUGS • WOODBURNERS

Introducing an unexpected twist on a classic decorating palette or scheme is a smart way to create intrigue and impact in a space. When I visited the tiny Italian island of Burano, it was this same feeling of surprise that left me inspired. Although located close to the grandeur of Venice, with its muted and romantic faded pink tones and neutral hues, this small isle couldn't be further away in terms of appearance, thanks to its array of boldly colourful buildings. It was this surprising hit of hue in an otherwise neutral environment that made me explore the notion of injecting bright colours into classic country spaces.

If you wish to introduce colour into a rustic space, take inspiration from the weathered patina of buildings then introduce colour and texture in one hit via painted and distressed wooden furniture. Allow the fearless, mix-and-match approach of the painted houses that line the canals in Burano to be the catalyst for a vibrant and cheerful Moroccan Boucherouite rug that is tempered by a taupe sofa and tufted ottoman-style coffee table. Try accenting dark neutral walls with a statement pendant light in a bright blue or yellow to make the whole room pop.

You can also experiment with a measured amount of clashing colour. Try injecting a bright red metal cabinet against a yellow wall, or allow a green cushion to intervene on a rich blue velvet chair for instance.

BOLD AND BEAUTIFUL

Going all out with hue in a country scheme can result in design dividends: a fireplace flue and surround painted in true blue (above right, top) looks striking against the terracotta floor tiles. For a warm look, opt for golden yellow and pair with rich red textiles (above left, top) to create a traditional feel, or rustic wooden furniture (above, bottom) for a more pastoral feel.

COUNTRY QUIRKS

Colour is one of the main decorating elements that can help to bring an unexpected twist to any dream space. When it came to decorating his Upstate New York weekend home, Martin Bourne had the aim of capitalizing on his knack for idiosyncratic decor touches in order to create an unexpected country home. Eschewing the expected shabby chic style of the property, Martin decided instead to fill the space with bold hues and personal pieces.

The dining room benefits from a long black table foiled by a series of mix and match chairs, including classic Bentwood chairs and simple folding metal designs. Their common thread is the saturated shades in which they are finished, from hot pink to sunshine yellow. Brushed metal pendant shades, beige curtains and a peppering of small artworks and colourful ceramics, vases and trays complement the rough wooden walls of the space.

HOT HUES
Brightly coloured dining chairs bring a surprising twist to this home in Upstate New York. A long wooden dining table and repeated hanging metal pendants help to visually elongate the room.

Brightly patterned tiles are a great way to visually anchor a large item into the rest of the decorating scheme.

FIREPLACE FOCUS

The fireplaces of these two rooms in an Upstate New York country home become the focus of their respective schemes thanks to eye-catching patterned tiles placed behind them. A yellow fire surround (above) serves as a frame to the woodburner in front, while a large flue extends upwards drawing the eye up to a metal starburst light (opposite).

COUNTRY IDYLL

Natural light streams into the rustic wooden kitchen of this American home. A metal farmhouse sink and freestanding trolley complete the casual country vibe.

KITCHEN ESSENTIALS

A well-functioning kitchen has everything to hand via smartly displayed items that offer both aesthetic and practical elements to the space. Here a wraparound open shelf houses a line-up of cake domes, baking dishes, mixing bowls and food storage. Overhead pendants are supported by a table lamp so that both everyday task lights, plus atmospheric lighting for a more relaxed mood, are available in the space.

COOK'S WHITES
An edit of cool, milky-white stoneware and ceramic cookware brings a fresh look to the shelves of this Upstate NY country kitchen (above top and bottom). A vase of freshly cut blooms softens the space, while classic red and white linens spell a charming country story (above, top).

COOL KITCHEN

A wooden sideboard, freestanding preparation trolley and open shelves bring a laid-back, welcoming feel to this country kitchen. Grey painted cabinetry adds a certain depth against the white walls.

FOUR STEPS TO COLOURFUL COUNTRY LIVING

01: UNEXPECTED HUE The green painted window frames of this country kitchen break up the all-white walls and create a visual frame for the soft natural light that floods into the space. This also provides a reference point to invite organic touches, such as cut blooms from the garden, into the scheme.

02: TERRIFIC TILES A leather Moroccan pouf and charcoal sofa are offset by striking blue and yellow tiles that create a focal point out of the fireplace in this dark and cocooning living room. Brunette wood panelling makes the colours of the tiles pop in the room.

03: HOT SEAT Introducing colour through sunshine-hued dining chairs, along with incidental touches such as a pink rose, help to add colour to a country space. Painted portraits lend a personal and comfortable tone to the playful colours, while a hung empty frame adds interest and intrigue.

04: PAINTED BEAUTY Painting the wooden walls of this bedroom blue all over creates a colourful yet calm feeling in the space. A red bedspread, which in turn is tempered by a Jute rug underfoot and a small bare wooden stool, accent the blue.

BRIGHT SPARK
A crisp white armchair
and vivid orange
and pink bedspread
punctuates the dark
racing green walls of
this American bedroom.
Connecting this space to
a master bathroom is a
sliding barn-style door.

HOLLYWOOD CHIC

inspired by Santa Barbara, California

No matter how often I visit Southern California I always find myself mesmerized by the softness of the light. It's a light that feels almost tangible, especially at the golden hour, when it glows with such warmth and intensity. At this time of day the decorative elements of small towns such as Santa Barbara on the Californian coast really come alive. The multi-coloured Spanish tiling shines brightly under the sun's rays and the gentle sway of the palms above create delicate shadow patterns on the ground. The terracotta shades of the tiled roofs become ever more pronounced and the colours of the sky transform from apricot to pink as the ocean beneath turns from azure blue to an inky midnight navy. It's these enchanting colours, patterns and textures that are the leading stars of the Hollywood Chic design style.

THE SPANISH COLONIAL INFLUENCES OF SANTA BARBARA
AND THE EXOTIC BLUE AND GREEN HUES OF SOUTHERN
CALIFORNIA SIT AT THE HEART OF THE HOLLYWOOD CHIC
STYLE. FROM COLOURFUL TILING WITH GRAPHIC FLORAL
MOTIFS TO ADOBE–INSPIRED INTERIOR DETAILING THERE
IS ALWAYS A NOD TO THE CONSTANT GOLDEN TONES
THAT INFLUENCE THE LIGHT AND ATMOSPHERE OF THE
'SUNSHINE' STATE.

RECIPE FOR HOLLYWOOD CHIC

WOOD PANELLING · SPANISH TILES · CLUB CHAIRS · STUDDED GLAMOROUS WALLPAPER · INTENSE TURQUOISE AND MIDNIGHT BLUE · MARBLE · STATEMENT GLASS LIGHTING · BRASS TOUCHES

The lure of Southern California and its laid-back, sun-soaked lifestyle is ever-present for me, so I knew I had to explore this part of the world to discover the decorating inspiration that allowed me to bring home the LA vibe. The result was the Hollywood Chic decor style, which takes its influences from Santa Barbara and the surrounding exotic beauty of Southern California. The vibrant and energizing colours and patterns of Spanish tiles are a great catalyst for inspiration when it comes to choosing floor materials and rug patterns for this glamorous and cheerful look.

Hollywood Chic encompasses an air of opulence and luxury too, alongside the classic Spanish Colonial decorating notes. Take inspiration from the intense midnight blue ocean at the golden hour and translate this into a dramatic blue wallpaper to create a cosy and cocooning dining space. Play with elements of a cool, clubby atmosphere to lift a hacienda vibe to a level of sleek sophistication. Inject opulence into such a scheme by introducing metallic and reflective finishes: studded wallpaper, a mirrored bar cart or brass wall lights for instance. In the same way that a Hollywood film has a leading star, ensure that every room has a statement feature, such as a piece of oversized original art, a light fitting or a dramatic or luxurious item of furniture. Look at using fabrics such as velvet and leather on upholstery and create impact with sophisticated floor tiling in hallways.

LUXE LIFESTYLE

Evoke the luxury feel of a Hollywood Hills home via a pair of statement zebra-print armchairs (above left, top) or a generously proportioned glass coffee table placed above an oversized ombré rug (above right). Play with black furniture to create a sense of drama and intrigue in a living space (above left, bottom).

CLUBHOUSE LIVING

When actor Jesse Tyler Ferguson and his lawyer husband, Justin Mikita moved into their Los Feliz home in the Hollywood Hills, they already had in mind the design aesthetic that they wished to inject into the space. While keen to maintain the Spanish Colonial features of the property, including many intricate and beautifully tiled floors, they also took inspiration from the decor direction of several Soho House creative clubs. This fusion of styles has resulted in a striking, elegant and refined space that has taken on a subtle, lived-in look to create a home that feels glamorous, grand and charismatic, yet welcoming at the same time.

LIBRARY ROOM

A tufted tan leather sofa and pair of brown leather armchairs face one another to create a comfortable reading area in the library of this Hollywood home. A brass bar cart adds a touch of luxury and echoes the two reading lamps.

CREATING INTIMACY IN BIG SPACES

A big interior can sometimes feel like more of a decor nightmare than a decor dream. However, this vast living room in a Los Angeles home is a prime example of how to transform a large, lofty area into a cosy, comfortable and cocooning space. A central snug area has been created by using a Moroccan Berber rug to anchor two neutral sofas dressed in colourful Jonathan Adler textiles. These reference a pair of ornately patterned armchairs, while an iron and glass coffee table is outfitted with personal mementos. An oversized circular light provides an intimate atmosphere.

COMFORTABLY GRAND
Jesse Tyler Ferguson and his husband, Justin Mikita, married comfort and grand style in the living room (opposite) of their Los Feliz home in Los Angeles, California. A large horse sculpture made entirely from old car parts adds grandeur to the central arch window, the commanding feeling of which is emphasised via an oversized mirror above the fireplace. A central hanging pendant creates comfort in the space, while vintage pieces, such as a typewriter (above) add interest and personality.

Juxtaposing large decorating elements with smaller design touches in a generous space helps to create a balanced room.

FOUR WAYS TO
UP THE LUXE

01: MATERIAL GIRL A focus on quietly luxurious materials lends a gently indulgent feel to this Los Angeles kitchen. Crisp white marble stretches the perimeter of the space, while solid built-in white cabinetry makes it feel spacious and airy. Wood-effect wallpaper adds texture to the far wall and the repetition of industrial metal pendants emphasizes the generous length of the central wooden table.

02: METALLIC TOUCH In contrast to the kitchen, the formal dining room of Jesse and Justin's LA home is dark and brooding in style. Midnight-blue wallpaper with brass studs adorns all four walls, and a mirrored console unit dressed in silverware and a vintage lamp help to continue the lavish style. Dark hardwood flooring mirrors the wooden panelled ceiling, further drawing the space inwards to create an intimate setting.

03: TREASURED FINDS Dream decor doesn't have to mean expensive outlays. Luxury is also delivered to a space via the personal pieces that carry a sentiment true only to you. Think: a vase of blooms that match those you had on your wedding day; a trinket box gifted to you by your grandparents, or found at a flea market on a first date. Decorate your home with the things you love and cherish to create personal luxury.

04: SITTING BEAUTY A tightly buttoned ochre leather sofa paired with a brass floor lamp and mirrored side table tell an instantly indulgent design story in the library of this Californian home. A circus-style arrow light injects a dash of unexpected whimsy, while the rich pink-red floor tiling completes the dream decor look of this Spanish Colonial home.

DRAMATIC DECOR

If ever there is a room in which to
decorate with drama it is a formal
dining room. As this is a space used
less frequently than say, a bedroom
or a living room, you can afford to
have fewer parameters around your
approach to the decor. In other words:
you can go all out with scale, pattern,
colour and textures to create maximum
impact. This divine dining space in the
Hollywood Hills home of Jesse Tyler
Ferguson and Justin Mikita does exactly
that. An incredible handmade glass
pendant light gives presence and pomp
to the dining table below. Vintage-style
brass wall lights add glamour to dark
navy wallpaper, while two mirrored
consoles and side lamps create stylish
symmetry either side of long and
luxurious window curtains.

CENTRE STAGE
In this Los Angeles dining
room, a series of glass
bells grouped together
into a statement pendant
take centre stage above
the leather dining chairs
around the long wooden
table below.

OUTSIDE LIVING

Outside space is on many dream decor location lists, but whether you have a tiny balcony, an everyday backyard or acres of land you can take inspiration from this stunning outdoor oasis in Los Angeles. Jesse Tyler Ferguson and Justin Mikita were keen to maximize the opportunity for outdoor living offered by their home in Southern California. To do so, they created several zones around a central pool area that tumbles down the hillside of the Hollywood property. For the decor elements, the duo took inspiration from their surroundings. The azure blue colour of the pool and sky is reflected in the Spanish pool tiling and painted window frames and doors. Elsewhere, a pair of wicker armchairs for reading are dressed in colourfully striped cushions to mirror the blooming bougainvillea behind. If you don't have an expanse of outdoor space to decorate, you can still dress it up. Create charm and intimacy by stringing cafe light bulbs above, place a handful of colourful planters on the decking and, if space allows, set up a small running water feature to induce a calming vibe.

EXOTIC BLISS
A split-level pool area (opposite) provides a tonic to the Southern Californian heat at this Los Angeles property. Other outdoor areas are dressed with succulents, a string of cafe bulbs and a fire pit (right, bottom). A pair of white armchairs provide a great reading spot (right, top).

INDOORS, OUTDOORS
An upholstered sofa, outdoor rug, cocktail table and pair of armchairs emulate an interior living space on the outdoor deck of this Hollywood Hills home, creating the perfect spot for alfresco entertaining and relaxing.

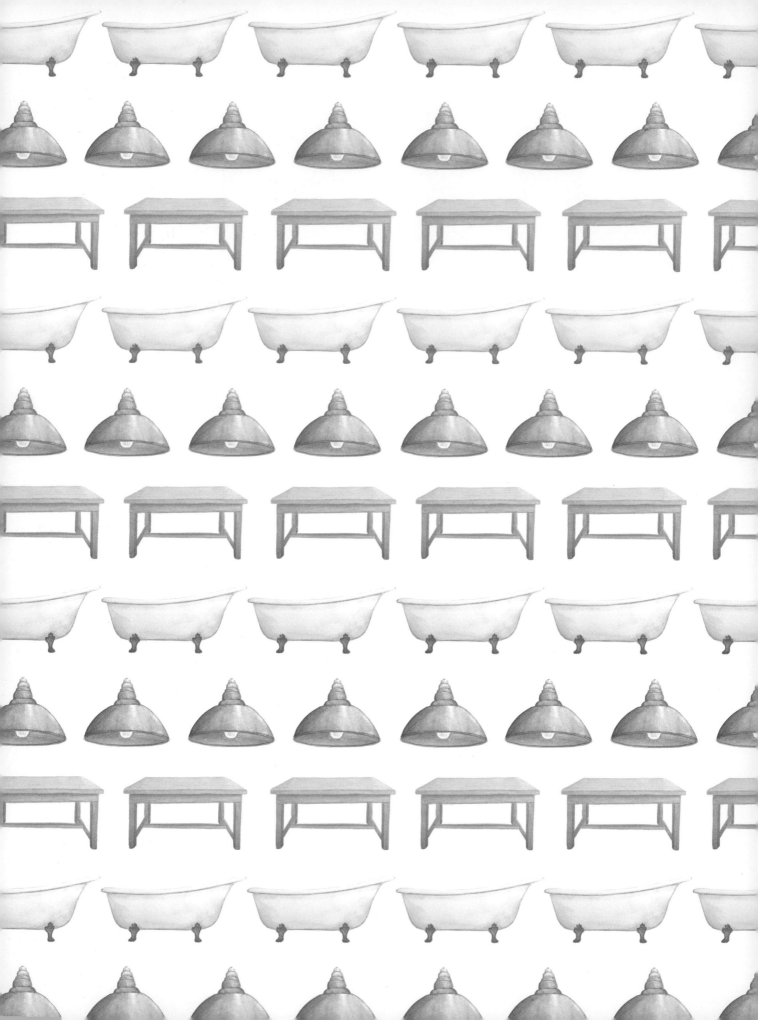

COOL COUNTRY

inspired by Sonoma, California

As I drove out of San Francisco towards Sonoma Wine Country I noticed how the metropolitan grip of the city transformed into wide open countryside. Tightly packed residential roads and towering skyscrapers gave way to dense forests and sweeping vineyards. Crossing the arresting industrial might of the Golden Gate Bridge marked a farewell to the colourful hues of San Francisco, and the start of the rustic, tactile and organic textures and shapes I would find in Sonoma. On arrival in the Wine Country, I headed for Scribe Winery, where the pastoral decor direction mirrored the surrounding vines and natural scenery. It was this journey that inspired me to think of a dream decor style that married elements from both city and country. The result? Cool Country: an inspiring fusion of city grit and country calm.

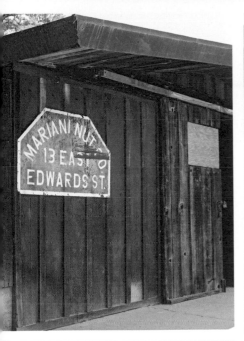

THE RUSTIC TEXTURES OF THIS SONOMA, CA VINEYARD INSPIRED A COUNTRY DECOR STYLE OOZING WITH COOL DESIGN DETAILS AND PASTORAL CHARM. HAVING SPENT MY EARLY CHILDHOOD LIVING IN THE COTSWOLDS, ENGLAND I WAS WELL VERSED IN CLASSIC COUNTRY STYLE. IT WAS THE UNEXPECTED DECORATING TWISTS I ENCOUNTERED AT STYLISH VINEYARDS THAT HELPED ME MIX COUNTRY AND COOL URBAN STYLES.

RECIPE FOR
COOL COUNTRY

WHITE WALLS · BLACK FLOORS · RECLAIMED FACTORY PENDANTS
BARE WOOD AND METAL · CURATED PIECES · HEXAGONAL TILES
EDISON BULBS · INDUSTRIAL FURNITURE · CLAW-FOOT BATHTUB

To emulate this cool country vibe, my advice is to take inspiration from layers of aged wood textures. For example, the look and feel of wooden fermentation barrels could inspire a headboard clad in reclaimed wood, while a sliding barn door could be introduced as a practical way to divide two rooms in a small space – a smart approach if you are looking to introduce a country atmosphere into a tight city apartment. While bringing untreated, rustic wood into a scheme will help to give a cooler vibe than, say, shabby chic furniture, you can go even further to mix up classic country style. Try layering in harder metal elements, such as factory pendants or iron-framed furniture to give more edge to a rustic scheme.

To take a country interior away from the simple, introduce other classic decorating twists that originate in the city or that emulate factory chic. Paint floors black instead of leaving them natural and neutral perhaps, then combine them with pure white walls, or introduce one-off pieces that bring an eclectic edge, such as reclaimed glass-fronted factory cabinets or repurposed furniture.

Mixing materials is also key to cool country, so seek out metal cabinets, glass-fronted cupboards or steel and wood tables to create an instant visual edge. These help steer the style away from any 'twee' connotations, so the look can work equally well in the city as it does in the country.

RURAL EDGE

Creating the dream of a comfortable country escape can be achieved, wherever you live, by incorporating a series of classic bucolic decor elements: a traditional white roll-top bathtub (above left) is an instant cue for cool country style, while a log store made from industrial iron (above right) lends an urban cutting edge to a pastoral space.

SCHOOLHOUSE RENOVATION

Leanne Ford and Brad Shaffer spent two years renovating this 1907 one-room schoolhouse in Pittsburgh, PA in order to make it their home. Having gathered furniture for years, the couple were thrilled to finally have a house of their own in which to house their collection. Although they picked up a brass trunk for £33 ($50) at a yard sale on their road the very day they moved in, they didn't rush the decor. Instead, they 'listened to' and observed their new home to see what style felt right for the house. The duo wanted to keep the mass of wood and imperfect, undone details in place, while also mixing in industrial details. They ripped off the drywall to expose original beadboard from the schoolhouse underneath. Next they took the wooden floors back to their original state and stained them dark to contrast with the largely white palette that runs throughout the property.

COUNTRY LIVING

To the homeowners of this renovated Pittsburgh schoolhouse, having a fireplace in the living room was central to their idea of dream decor in the country. They paired it with an exposed bulb light pendant and industrial wooden coffee table.

The Woodard chairs were
chosen to go around
the dining table in this
Pennsylvanian home (left)
because they matched the
large metal pendant, but
they are also durable enough
to be used outdoors during
the summer months. In the
kitchen, a farmhouse sink
was placed in front of the
window to make the most
of the country views, while
factory pendants suspended
from the ceiling provide task
lighting to a central wooden
island unit. Matt white
subway tiles successfully
inject a splash of urbanity
to the scheme (opposite).

DINING WITH MEMORIES

For the couple that lives in this country home in Pittsburgh, each dinnertime is
truly like dining with treasured memories. Their kitchen table was a wedding gift
that was handmade and gifted to the couple by a group of close friends. They used
it as the communion table on their wedding day, then it was used as the DJ table,
and now it's in the heart of their home and functions as the kitchen table.

THREE WAYS TO INFUSE COOL INTO COUNTRY

01: MARVELLOUS MARBLE
Replicate the cool and shiny-floored lobbies of contemporary skyscrapers via a marble-topped bedside table. It will contrast beautifully with bare wood textures. Or place a mirrored table lamp on top, for an unexpected dash of city chic amid a rustic interior.

02: INDUSTRIAL APPEAL
Team up classic country decor directions, such as open wooden shelves in the kitchen, with lighting solutions reclaimed from old factories. Keep pipework and the original ceiling on show to add grit to the country charm. Sticking within a white palette creates a cohesive space that sits comfortably with a countryside location.

03: CENTRE POINT
The owners of this renovated schoolhouse in Pittsburgh, PA strung a series of traditional Edison bulbs from lighting cord around a metal ring in order to create a central focal point in the living room (right).

WHITE OUT

In renovating a 1907 schoolhouse in Pennsylvania a couple created an all-white bathroom (this page) peppered with cool design notes such as an industrial swivel stool that sits alongside gathered finds, including a weathered wooden mirror (opposite).

BATHED IN CONTRAST

A chic monochromatic palette sets the tone for the country cool design direction of Leanne and Brad's master bathroom in their Pittsburgh, PA home. Set in the eaves of the schoolhouse, they painted the wooden ceiling white and then tiled throughout: the floors in a hexagonal pattern; the walls in subway tiling. The fresh white palette is accented with metallic and black design details. A traditional white claw foot bathtub sits beneath brass taps, which in turn tie in with the double shower fittings opposite. Wooden shutters are painted jet black to frame the picture window that looks out over the surrounding woodland.

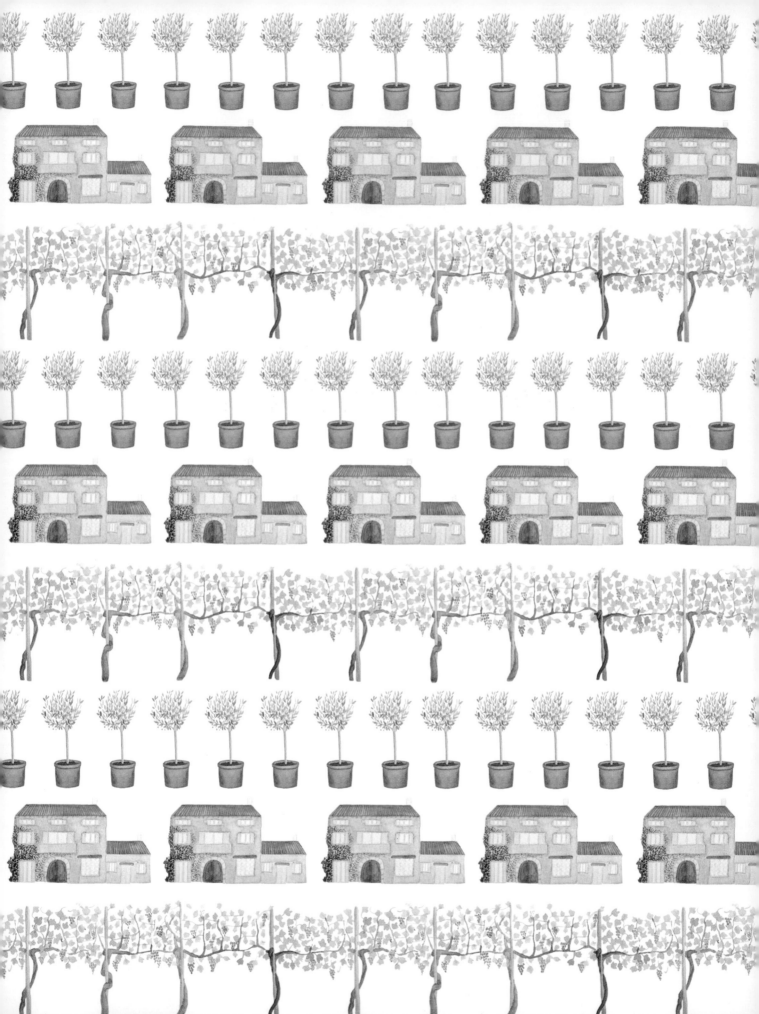

ITALIAN RUSTIC

inspired by Tuscany, Italy

Hiring a car and driving through the Tuscan hills in Italy proved to be a trip full of design inspiration. Sweeping hillsides were graced with cypress trees planted in perfect lines that curved in sync with the roads as they appeared to navigate up and down the various valleys. Ancient Italian towns, such as Cortona in Arezzo, where the medieval architecture that lined the steep narrow streets, left me inspired to consider designs that make a grand statement out of simple materials. Much like Italian food, where classic, simple ingredients are often paired to make delicious meals – rustic Italian style involves putting together simple materials like wood and brick which join forces to make design statements. This particular style favours natural decor elements in order to create dream spaces that remain in style forever.

TRADITIONAL STONE BUILDINGS, OLIVE GROVES AND CYPRESS TREES AS FAR AS THE EYE COULD SEE IN TUSCANY INSPIRED THE ITALIAN RUSTIC DREAM DECOR STYLE. THIS UNMISTAKEABLE LOOK IS THE RESULT OF HONEYED TERRACOTTA TONES INDOORS AND OUT, OCHRE WALLS PERFECTLY PUNCTUATED WITH DEEP OLIVE PAINTED SHUTTERS AND NATURAL GREENERY. THESE ALL TONE BEAUTIFULLY WITH WHITE WALLS AND ROUGH-TEXTURED CERAMICS, BOTH AT THE TABLE AND IN THE GARDEN.

RECIPE FOR
ITALIAN RUSTIC

WHITEWASHED STONE AND BRICK · CONCRETE QUARTZ FLOOR
TERRACOTTA · PATTERNED ENCAUSTIC TILES · POPS OF YELLOW
ORGANIC GREENS · OLD FILM REELS · DISTRESSED PAINTED WOOD

What I love about interior design is its ability to completely change the atmosphere of a space simply by means of the decorating elements you choose to bring into the room. I kept this in mind during a trip to Tuscany in Italy: here I was determined to seek out inspiration and ideas to take the effortlessly cool, tactile and stylish vibe of rustic Italian properties into a home anywhere else in the world.

I soon discovered that the key to emulating this timeless decorating style was to focus on sensory experiences while exploring the rolling Tuscan hills. Inviting the outdoors in could be achieved via vases filled with olive branches and freshly pulled lemons; inspiration could be taken from the painted wooden shutters that adorn the outside of countless traditional Tuscan buildings to inspire the colour of a statement piece of furniture; the gnarled and twisted branches in endless olive groves could serve as the catalyst for a beautifully tactile, bare wood kitchen table; or the stone buildings become a steering point for the smooth, timeless and cooling material that should be used for occasional furniture. Whitewashing stone walls and exposed brick is a great way of providing a bright, refreshing base on which to layer the natural textures and colours that signify Italian Rustic style – chalky blue and terracotta tones, pops of bright colour and a relaxed, inviting vibe in which less is more.

TUSCAN SUNSHINE

Natural textures are some of the quickest decorating tools to use for introducing Tuscan style in to your home. Keep walls, floors and ceilings exposed and consider flagstone floors (above left, top) underfoot; rich orange, earth or red colour palettes (above right) as accents; and by decorating with simple displays of pottery and ceramics (above left).

SERENE STYLE

A heaven of serenity. That's how the owner and designer likes to describe this weekend home in the southern Italian region of Puglia. The architect, Raffaele Centonze, designed the house to be a refuge; a place for him, his wife, Francesca and their children, Lorenzo and Claudia to escape the stress and noise of everyday city life. Raffaele took a 'less is more' approach to the design of the interior, choosing to mix organic elements like bamboo and driftwood, with found vintage pieces such as old cinematic film wheels. Splashes of exotic hue punctuate the neutral stone and concrete quartz floor, and warmth is added via bare wooden furniture.

NATURAL DESIGN
The dining space of this Italian country home is furnished with a reclaimed wooden table, old school chairs and a distressed azure blue sideboard. Gathered driftwood sits upon the polished concrete floor to fill an empty nook.

FAMILY TIME
A long wooden table is perfect for allowing the Centonze family to enjoy long lunches with loved ones in the dining room of their Puglia home.

UNDERSTATED STYLE

Raffaele and Francesca's dining room is a lesson in taking a 'less is more' approach to dream decor. A cool white interior and polished concrete quartz floor was the basis for the dining space in their weekend home; a haven from the intense Mediterranean heat. Simple splashes of mint green painted on chairs complement the long, bucolic wooden table.

ARCHITECTURAL VISION
The view through an elegant archway to the dining space of this Italian home (above) frames the elements of the interior within the room. A trio of glass pendant lamps hang at either end of the room, pairing with the painted wooden chairs. A vintage table lamp brings height to the rustic chest, which functions as a sideboard.

BRING HOME ITALIAN RUSTIC STYLE IN FOUR STEPS

01: BARE IS BEST Unfinished materials lend a pastoral feel to a room, as shown in the bedroom of this Italian home. A door made from wooden planks lends tactility, warmth and colour to the fresh white interior. Keep everything simple – a non-patterned bedspread, uncluttered furniture and a clear floor space.

02: ORGANIC ELEMENTS A rustic vibe can be introduced by bringing the outdoors in. A gathered bunch of blooms and fruit instantly spells laid-back Italian style. Think: lemons fresh from the tree, fragrant lavender and vibrant green leaves. Place the greenery in a white vase to keep the display looking pared-back and unassuming.

03: FOCUS ON TEXTURE Encaustic tiles
work well in a kitchen because the pattern on
the surface of the tiles is not a glaze, but rather
formed of different colours of clay. As the pattern
is inlaid into the tile it remains, even when the
tiles wear down, so a lovely texture remains.
These brown and ochre designs complement the
reclaimed wooden kitchen units and shelving.

04: TERRACOTTA HUES This unique
bathroom colour dates back many centuries in
the region of Puglia. The 'cooked earth' look is
achieved by adding plaster to earthenware clay,
which is then crushed into small pieces and fired
to give a rich orange hue. Try replicating this
with bathroom paint, applying it so that it has a
distressed, mottled effect for a more unique look.

RUSTIC & REFINED

A blend of sophisticated simplicity, achieved by mixing vintage and rural decor elements, creates a striking living room in the Centonze's weekend home. The chimney (opposite) was designed by Raffaele and is adorned with an arched iron fanlight that he found in an old house in the historic centre of Lecce. The walls and the vaults of the space are painted in white lime, with the whitewash helping to disguise the rough bricks. This colour is referenced in the stools that were sculpted out of local stone. A lamp made from a birdcage, and a driftwood collection washed up from the Adriatic Sea, offer a gently pastoral finishing touch.

CULTIVATED DESIGN
Film coils (above) were recovered from an old cinema located in the historic centre of Lecce. Between the two stone stools (opposite) sits a brazier from the early 1900s – originally used to hold hot coals, it now functions as a coffee table in this home in Puglia, Italy. A distressed chest adds colour and texture (right).

A focus on introducing just a handful of considered designs in a 'less is more' approach to dream decor results in a striking space.

PETITE PARISIENNE

inspired by Paris, France

Arguably, no other city has an intoxicating power quite like Paris. From the chic inhabitants of the metropolis, each clad head-to-toe in black and Breton stripes, to the arresting architecture and heady smells wafting from corner boulangeries, it's impossible not to find a trip to the 'city of light' an inspiring experience. These intense sensory experiences are at the heart of why I find travel so inspirational in my design and styling work. It's in these moments that I have an overpowering desire to bottle up a colour, a texture or a pattern and bring it home with me. In Paris I found an unexpected dichotomy that captured my design thoughts: although the city often has a grand exterior, many of the interiors, from homes to restaurants, are petite in comparison. This inspired me to seek out an interior style that showed – in spite of limited space – what Parisians do best: effortless chic.

THE PLAY ON STYLE AND SCALE BETWEEN THE ELEVATED ROMANCE AND GRANDEUR OF PARIS AGAINST THE CITY'S SMALL, QUAINT AND COSY ENVIRONMENTS LED ME TO DEVELOP THE PETITE PARISIENNE LOOK. CREATING A POCKET OF COMFORTABLE CHIC LIVING IS VITAL IN A CITYSCAPE WHERE SPACE IS AT A PREMIUM, SO THE EMPHASIS IS ON CREATING A SENSE OF AIR AND LIGHT, EVEN IN A TINY URBAN APARTMENT.

RECIPE FOR
PETITE PARISIENNE

IRON STAIRCASE · HANGING EDISON BULBS · LINEN-COVERED SOFA
BARE BRICK WALLS · WOODEN BEAMS · EAMES CHAIRS · STAINLESS
STEEL CABINETRY · RETRO MIRRORS · MOROCCAN SOUK-STYLE RUG

Millions call Paris the most romantic city in the world and it's this vision of the French metropolis that often leads to the notion that its interiors are therefore equally romanticized. After numerous trips to the 'city of light', I started to notice a juxtaposition between the scale of the city's impressive architecture – not least the world famous Eiffel Tower – against the quieter, cozier moments experienced in Paris' tiny cafes, shops, streets and restaurants. This led me to consider a Parisian-inspired interior which harnessed this dichotomy to create an unexpected dream decor style.

Being open to the differing sights and experiences of Paris – from grand to quiet – you can create an intriguing and stylish space. For example, the industrial might of the Eiffel Tower can be the spark for a custom iron staircase that becomes an architectural statement all of its own on a much smaller scale in a small, open-plan apartment. Translating the grandeur of the city into a small space can also be achieved by introducing delicate decorating touches. For example, rather than a series of three grand 'statement' light pendants, you can achieve a chic, subtle look that still has an industrial twist by hanging three bare Edison bulbs. Simple.

By shoe-horning in stylish storage solutions to disguise clutter and creating an interesting mix of materials you can help to divert attention away from the fact that space is limited in such a busy city.

IRON STYLE

Inject an air of cool dream decor style with a Parisian twist into a scheme via a series of iron elements. Fitting a traditional radiator and painting it black (above, top) creates a contrast against exposed bricks. Introducing design classics, such as a Barcelona chair (above, right) or a set of Eames dining chairs (above, left) creates a sophisticated space.

STYLISH STUDIO LIVING

For French television presenter Marine Vignes and her family, small space doesn't mean small style. On finding the deserted warehouse space in the 18th arrondissement of Paris, Marine decided to buy two ground floor units, knocking through the entire space to create one large room out of a series of tiny rooms. Taking her lead from the existing features of the building exposed bricks and the wooden beams uncovered from the ceiling plaster – she undertook the design and layout of the apartment herself. The result is an ingeniously designed space that zones one space into areas for cooking, dining, sleeping and living – all tied together via an unexpected theme for a Parisian apartment. cool industrial style.

RAW MATERIALS

The design story of this apartment in Paris, France is told via a focus on raw materials, from rough uncovered bricks and smooth metal doors, to exposed wooden beams and a bespoke iron staircase.

DESIGNING A CHIC PETITE INDUSTRIAL INTERIOR

01: METAL MOMENTS Use metal to create prominent design moments in a space; it's a material that can help create ebb and flow in a room by breaking a linear aesthetic. Here a custom iron staircase creates an arresting architectural moment. It seamlessly ties in with the stainless steel kitchen cabinetry, while also providing a textural change to the rough wooden beams and bricks that dominate the space.

02: GENEROUS PROPORTIONS By upsizing everything in this open-plan living, dining and sleeping space in Paris, the result is a space that feels bigger than it is. By keeping the number of items to a minimum but the size of each item generously proportioned, it gives an illusion of space. Tactile textures via soft linen furnishings add a chic touch against large metal windows.

03: BUILT-IN STORAGE Custom built-in wooden storage stretches the entire length of this open-plan studio living space in Paris. It helps to keep the concrete floor open and clutter-free, allowing for a clean line through all the various zones of the space. This again helps to give the apartment a sizable warehouse feel, while also giving plenty of opportunity to store and display personal keepsakes.

04: CONTRAST TEXTURES By dressing the bedroom area in delicately patterned textiles a contrast is created against the industrial aesthetic of the iron window frame. In this area of the apartment, the rough texture of the bricks is covered with a smooth, serene, white painted plaster. It's this simple change in material and finish that creates a new mood within one space.

SPLASHBACK SUPRISE
From afar the splashback of Marine Vignes' kitchen in Paris, France (above) looks like tiling, but up close it is actually metallic wallpaper that sits behind a sheet of clear glass.

RETRO FUSION
In this open-plan kitchen-dining space, an animal hide successfully softens a classic Eames dining chair, while a trio of wooden mirrors continues the subtle retro vibe (opposite).

Focus on contrasting materials, such as hard metals teamed with soft cork and linen, to create a cool yet comfortable interior.

LAID-BACK
An air of effortless cool is created in this French home by dressing an inviting day bed with layers of cushions and throws in a tonal green colour palette.

SYSTEMATIC STYLE

In this Parisian bedroom a methodical approach to the interior design means that the space is uncluttered and orderly, allowing for a restful night's sleep. A metal locker functions as a bedside table, while a bed dressed generously in linens creates comfort amongst the harder industrial decor.

SCANDI COMFORT

inspired by the Arctic Circle, Finland

The moment I looked out of the window as we flew over the Baltic Sea and saw the most incredible winter sunset I knew that my trip deep into the Arctic Circle was going to be full of inspiring experiences. Waiting for me when I landed was the sight of log cabins with snow-capped roofs and roaring woodburners, nestled amongst the trees in the forest, while hanging lanterns lined snow-covered paths that led down to frozen lakes. Reindeer roamed through the trees and candles flickered from the windows of each cabin. By day everything felt crisp, fresh and invigorating thanks to the clear blue skies and abundance of snow and ice. By nightfall it was the auroras in the inky night sky that majestically brought bursts of hue into the white landscape. Seeing the Northern Lights for the first time led me to consider an interior style that married the cool, comfortable whites of a traditional Scandinavian home with intermittent flashes of exciting colour.

THE INVIGORATING EXPERIENCE OF A
HUSKY SLEIGH RIDE ACROSS FROZEN
LAKES AND THROUGH FORESTS OF SNOW-
CAPPED TREES IN FINLAND INSPIRED
THE COOL WHITES AT THE HEART OF THE
SCANDI COMFORT DECORATING STYLE.
AGAINST THE COOL WHITE BACKDROP
OF NATURE AND PAINTED WOODEN
INTERIORS, SCANDI COMFORT ALSO
INVOLVES A SENSITIVE MELDING OF
SOFT BLUES WITHIN THE PALE PALETTE.

RECIPE FOR SCANDI COMFORT

ALL-WHITE WALLS · BLUE AND WHITE ACCESSORIES · GRID TILES
UNDRESSED WINDOWS · LOOSE LINEN COVERS · BRUSHED METAL
FLOOR LAMPS · STRIPES AND CHECKS · HERRINGBONE FLOORS

I've always admired the ability of Scandinavians to achieve such effortlessly relaxed, inviting and comfortable spaces – and seemingly using so few elements, too! When I took a trip deep into the Finnish Arctic Circle I was left inspired by the sheer beauty of the snow-laden landscape, and the welcoming comfort of the wooden cabin interiors. I knew that there were catalysts to be discovered in this captivating and magical winter environment that could be translated into an equally show-stopping chic and simple interior.

Scandinavia is covered in boundless forests, and Finland was no different. The beautiful texture of tree bark against the crisp white snowfall is a combination that also works back at home in an interior scheme. For example, deep sofas upholstered with loose-fit, white linen covers paired with a dark wooden coffee table offer a similar contrast between dark and light, soft and hard. The third element that sits at the heart of this Scandi style is also inspired by the natural environment: the sky. From the intense blues of the sky to the hint of blue in the snow, the abundance of blue shades offer inspiration for the perfect accent colour in a Scandi scheme. Layer in an array of blue hues across textiles, such as cushions, throws, rugs, bedding and kitchen accessories.

WHITE OUT

You can invite the beauty of a Scandinavian snowdrift into a home through an all-white palette. A scheme with milky white floors, walls, ceilings, soft furnishings and painted furniture (above, right) generates a crisp and fresh feel when punctuated with a splash of greenery. Opt for a creamier shade of white to create a warmer interior (above, left).

SCANDINAVIAN SENSIBILITIES

The founders of fashion and interiors brand, The Lexington Company, Kristina and Tommy Lindhe were keen to create a family home that reflected their love for classic, comfortable style. The couple's love of timeless East Coast American style didn't only inspire the name of their business, but their Swedish home, too. They took their Scandinavian sensibilities and fused it with a preppy New England vibe to create a cool, comfortable home that is decorated in a timeless blue and white colour palette throughout.

CALM COMFORT

A serene atmosphere is created in this home in a leafy suburb of Stockholm, Sweden thanks to inviting sofas with white linen slip covers, an abundance of natural light and a peppering of tactile blue and white textiles.

The entryway of this Swedish home (right) is simply furnished with an old whitewashed wooden table and striking red and white stripe curtains. A bunch of fresh hydrangeas nod to the family's enduring love of a relaxed New England lifestyle.

BALANCED LIVING

The Lindhe family decorated their home on the outskirts of Stockholm, Sweden with a considered mix of old and new pieces. Kristina likes to come home to a clean environment, so the home combines classic Swedish elements such as whitewashed wood with a simple blue and white colour scheme with splashes of red. A bare wooden floor is softened with a neutral, large-scale rug, while the scene is softened here and there with fresh flowers.

SCANDI STYLE
The plain linen sofas of this Swedish living room allow for checked and striped textiles to be layered in. A pair of brushed metal task floor lamps anchors the main seating area, which is centred on a dark wooden table.

FOUR STEPS TO STYLISH SCANDI SIMPLICITY

01: PEPPER IN PATTERNS A rudimentary pattern, such as a single stripe or repeated star emblems, can help inject life into an interior. Keeping the patterns simple and unfussy means the space feels lively and interesting but not cluttered or tiring on the eye.

02: OPEN UP Evoke the laid-back New England lifestyle that inspired this home in Sweden by opening up kitchen storage. Head-height open shelving creates a feeling of added space and a relaxed, grab-and-go atmosphere. Alternate these with frosted glass units so that you can still keep unsightly necessities to hand, but out of sight.

Add interest to a continuous palette by switching up the colour, pattern and textures you choose for each decor element.

03: LESS IS MORE By limiting what you bring into a scheme you will give yourself a kickstart in creating a streamlined and sophisticated final look. Two simple, white hanging cafe pendants anchor the slate-topped dining table inside this Swedish kitchen. It's this restrained approach to the decor that allows the hero natural feature of the space – wooden herringbone floors – to shine.

04: COHESIVE COLOUR No colour palette says 'calm, classic and comfortable' quite like blue and white. Picking a duo of hues and using them through a room or even a house will make it easier for you to create a consistent flow to the space. Mix up the use of patterns, materials and finishes to keep a repeat colour palette interesting.

SEASONAL CHANGE
Kristina designed the chandelier in the dining room of her Swedish family home so that she could decorate the focal point of the room with different plants as the seasons changed.

INDUSTRIAL LOFT

inspired by Shoreditch, London

London is a melting pot of diversity and creativity, but it's Shoreditch in the historic East End of London where this ever-present spirit in the city feels truly at home. The district is made up of many former factories and warehouses that tell a story of a now defunct industrial era. Flat-fronted architecture with expansive iron windows and lofty ceilings line many of the streets, its exposed bricks laid bare both internally and externally. The area's resourceful spirit stems from the largely creative inhabitants in the area. This has resulted in a rich mix of vintage furniture and industrial design that has fused together, due to several decades of gentrification, with modern and contemporary designs. Each time I visit I feel inspired to see how this synthesis of dream decorating elements can lead to unique loft living.

THE HISTORIC EAST END OF LONDON
AND ITS HUGE WAREHOUSE BUILDINGS
WITH METAL–FRAMED WINDOWS AND
EXPOSED BRICKS LED ME TO CONSIDER
AN INDUSTRIAL LOFT INTERIOR. WITH
PLENTY OF NATURAL LIGHT THANKS TO
'WALLS' OF WINDOWS AND INTERIOR
SPACES WHERE TEXTURE IS EVER PRESENT,
THE ESSENCE OF INDUSTRIAL CHIC LIES
IN SOFTENING AND BREAKING UP HARD
TEXTURES AND DARK COLOURS.

RECIPE FOR INDUSTRIAL LOFT

ROUGH METAL PENDANTS · EXPOSED BRICKS · COLLECTED GLASS
BOTTLES · INTERNAL IRON STRUCTURES · RECLAIMED LOCKERS
FOUND COGS AND WHEELS · SLIDING DOORS · VINTAGE SUITCASES

As the popularity of industrial style has continued to increase in recent years, so has my interest in this approach to decorating. Although popular as a vision of many people's dream decor, industrial style can often be considered unobtainable if you don't actually live in a warehouse or loft space. As I walked through the streets lined with industrial warehouses in Shoreditch, East London I was keen to think of ways to bring this look home, no matter where you live.

Focus on the classic industrial elements – metal, brick and glass – and refashion them for the space in mind. For example, if you live in a new build with smooth plastered walls, why not paper one wall with a brick effect wallpaper to evoke a loft-like atmosphere? Your furniture choices will also help to encourage a warehouse style. Opt for a low-lying coffee table with a wooden top and metal base, and then pair it with a display of collected glass russet and clear bottles with vintage labels to make for an eye-catching display. If you don't have space for tall metal lockers, introduce the same look via a small bedside table instead. Also, try collecting old cogs and wheels from flea markets and group them together above a sideboard or sofa as a nod to warehouse style.

Painted and repurposed factory workbenches, or re-constructed wooden pallets and wooden produce boxes also help to create the look.

DARK AND LIGHT

Create visual interest in an industrial scheme by playing with contrasts: smooth, white ceramics grouped upon a metal locker for instance (top right); a weathered brown leather sofa against polished concrete floors (above) or a reclaimed wooden table combined with striking brass light pendants (top left).

LOFT LIVING

The spotlight shines on modern, urban warehouse style living in this historical Yaletown loft in Vancouver, Canada. Owned by an A-list movie star and his actor wife, the property was renovated throughout and then decorated with both vintage and modern pieces that enhance the natural character of the listed building. Wooden beams expose the property's long heritage, while a metal bar linking a series of reclaimed spotlights and lighting hoods from old movie studios references the owners' careers as film actors. A weathered blue paint effect on the cabinetry adds hue to the linear kitchen, while herringbone tiling gives a graphic edge to the overall scheme.

KITCHEN COLOUR
An elongated island unit functions as a space for food preparation and eating in this Canadian kitchen. Colour is introduced to the loft space via painted wooden cabinets.

A LUXE TOUCH

The interior of this historical loft in Vancouver is given a surprising twist. Rather than play entirely on the existing industrial elements of the space, a series of glamorous additions were placed front and centre to create a unique living space. The statement fireplace was clad from floor to ceiling in copper to create a luxurious contrast against the brick walls and iron framework. A backlit drinks storage unit cleverly housed under the open stairs introduces an indulgent and romantic restaurant atmosphere into the kitchen area of the apartment.

INDUSTRIAL LOFT, THREE WAYS...

Gather heritage pieces from flea markets and scrap yards to build up an authentic industrial look.

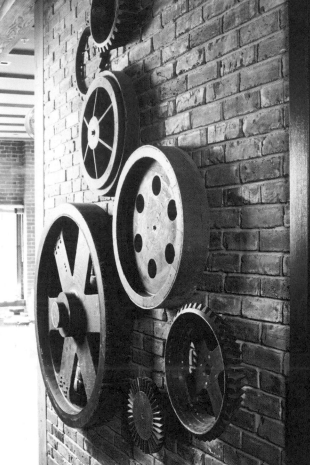

01: COOL COLOURS This historical loft in Vancouver's Yaletown district has a stylish tension between luxury modern elements and reclaimed textures. In this bathroom corrugated iron clad onto the wall is juxtaposed with high gloss fixtures and fittings, and glamorous teardrop glass wall lights.

02: WHEELS IN MOTION A collection of wheels and cogs are grouped together on an exposed brick wall to create an instantly industrial display, which adds visual interest to a narrow hallway.

03: LOCKER LOVE Metal lockers with a gorgeous green patina are repurposed as entryway storage. A collection of figurines provides a dash of whimsy amongst the harder elements.

REPURPOSED FINDS

A compendium of old glassware is arranged to create interest in the dining area (above) of this Canadian loft apartment. Meanwhile, vintage suitcases piled on top of one another serve as a quirky side table (opposite).

DREAM DECOR SOURCES AND CREDITS

LOCATION OWNERS

ANTHONY D'ARGENZIO
Lower East Side, NYC, USA
www.zioandsons.com

BENJAMIN STELLY
AND WILLIAM BUCKLEY
Harlem, NYC, USA
www.benjaminstelly.com

CHRIS O'SHEA
AND ASHBY DODGE
Bridgehampton, NY, USA
www.chrisosheaphotography.com

JESSE TYLER FERGUSON
AND JUSTIN MIKITA
Los Angeles, CA, USA
Interior design by Peter Gurski
www.petergurski.com

KRISTINA AND TOMMY LINDHE
Stockholm, Sweden
www.lexingtoncompany.com

LEANNE FORD
AND BRAD SHAFFER
Pittsburgh, PA, USA
www.leannefordinteriors.com
and *www.acrecreative.com*

MARINE VIGNES
Paris, France
TV Personality

MARTIN BOURNE
Dumbo, Brooklyn, NYC, USA &
Upstate NY, USA
*www.judycasey.com/prop-set-design/
martin-bourne*

RAFFAELE CENTONZE
Puglia, Italy
www.r100.it

WILL TAYLOR
London, United Kingdom
www.brightbazaarblog.com

UNDISCLOSED HOMEOWNER
Vancouver, Canada
Film star

URSULA MASCARO
Menorca, Spain
www.ursulamascaro.com

DREAM DECOR SOURCES

WALLS AND FLOORS

CLAESSON KOIVISTO RUNE
www.claessonkoivistorune.se

COLE & SON
www.cole-and-son.com

FIRED EARTH
www.firedearth.com

FERM LIVING
www.fermliving.com

MINI MODERNS
www.minimoderns.com

PHOTOWALL
www.photowall.co.uk

OSBORNE & LITTLE
www.osborneandlittle.com

WALLPAPER DIRECT
www.wallpaperdirect.com

FURNITURE

BLUEDOT
www.bluedot.com

BROOKLYN FLEA MARKET
www.brooklynflea.com

BY MAY
www.bymay.se

CB2
www.cb2.com

CRATE & BARREL
www.crateandbarrel.com

HAY
www.hay.dk

HOME BARN
www.homebarnshop.co.uk

JAYSON HOME
www.jaysonhome.com

JOHN LEWIS
www.johnlewis.com

LOAF
www.loaf.com

MADE
www.made.com

MECOX GARDENS
www.mecox.com

NEXT
www.next.com

SERENA & LILY
www.serenaandlily.com

SOFA.COM
www.sofa.com

THE CONRAN SHOP
www.theconranshop.co.uk

WAYFAIR
www.wayfair.com

TEXTILES

ABC CARPET & HOME
www.abchome.com

BEMZ
www.bemz.com

COUNTRY ROAD
www.countryroad.com.au

DESIGNERS GUILD
www.designersguild.com

ETSY
www.etsy.com

H&M HOME
www.hm.com

HABITAT
www.habitat.co.uk

FINE LITTLE DAY
www.finelittleday.com

LEXINGTON COMPANY
www.lexingtoncompany.com

LIBERTY
www.liberty.co.uk

MARIMEKKO
www.marimekko.com

REBECCA ATWOOD
www.rebeccaatwood.com

TARGET
www.target.com

TOAST
www.toa.st

WEST ELM
www.westelm.com

LIGHTING

BHS
www.bhs.co.uk

EBAY
www.ebay.com

IKEA
www.ikea.com

HEALS
www.heals.com

HOMEGOODS
www.homegoods.com

ONE KINGS LANE
www.onekingslane.com

POTTERY BARN
www.potterybarn.com

ROCKETT ST GEORGE
www.rockettstgeorge.co.uk

SCHOOLHOUSE ELECTRIC
www.schoolhouseelectric.com

SKANDIUM
www.skandium.com

TOM DIXON
www.tomdixon.net

PAINT

BENJAMIN MOORE
www.benjaminmoore.com

BEHR
www.behr.com

FARROW & BALL
www.farrow-ball.com

RALPH LAUREN
www.ralphlaurenhome.com

SHERWIN WILLIAMS
www.sherwin-williams.com

VALSPAR
www.valsparpaint.co.uk

ACCESSORIES

ANTHROPOLOGIE
www.anthropologie.com

CANVAS
www.canvashomestore.com

FISHS EDDY
www.fishseddy.com

HUDSON'S BAY
www.thebay.com

JONATHAN ADLER
www.jonathanadler.com

LEIF
www.leifshop.com

MERCI
www.merci-merci.com

MUD AUSTRALIA
www.mudaustralia.com

NOT ON THE HIGH STREET
www.notonthehighstreet.com

OLIVER BONAS
www.oliverbonas.com

PAPER SOURCE
www.papersource.com

PONYRIDER
www.ponyrider.com.au

SMUG
www.ifeelsmug.com

STEVEN ALAN HOME
www.stevenalan.com

SYLVESTER & CO.
www.sylvesterandco.com

TERRAIN
www.shopterrain.com

THE SOCIETY INC.
www.thesocietyinc.com.au

URBAN OUTFITTERS
www.urbanoutfitters.com

ZARA HOME
www.zarahome.com

ACKNOWLEDGEMENTS

The travel photographs in this book were taken by Will Taylor. All other photographs are by Andrew Boyd, apart from the following:
Page 20, 32: Photography by D. Gilbert, interior design by DISC Interiors. Page 42, 72, 82-3: Photography by Jonny Valiant, interior design by Robert Passal Interiors. Page 93 bottom right, Simon Upton/© Jacqui Small LLP, top right, Simon Upton/© Jacqui Small LLP; 121 top left Simon Upton/© Jacqui Small LLP, top right Simon Upton/© Jacqui Small LLP, bottom right Simon Upton/© Jacqui Small LLP; 121, bottom left, Simon Upton/© Jacqui Small LLP; 139 top left Simon Upton/© Jacqui Small LLP, bottom left Simon Upton/© Jacqui Small LLP, right Janis Nicolai/© Jacqui Small LLP; 153 top left, Simon Upton/© Jacqui Small LLP, bottom, Simon Upton/© Jacqui Small LLP, top right Simon Upton/© Jacqui Small LLP; 171 top left Ken Hayden/ © Jacqui Small LLP, bottom left Ken Hayden/© Jacqui Small LLP, right Andrew Wood/© Jacqui Small LLP; 189 right, Simon Upton/© Jacqui Small LLP; 203 top left Simon Upton/© Jacqui Small LLP, bottom left Simon Upton/© Jacqui Small LLP, right Simon Upton © Jacqui Small LLP; 217 top Debi Treloar © Jacqui Small LLP, bottom left Simon Upton/© Jacqui Small LLP, bottom right, Simon Upton/ © Jacqui Small LLP; 231 left Simon Upton/© Jacqui Small LLP, right, Simon Upton/© Jacqui Small LLP; 242 top right © Joanna Copestick/Very English Ltd; 242 bottom right Michael Sinclair © Jacqui Small LLP; 245 top left Simon Upton/© Jacqui Small LLP, top right Janis Nicolai/© Jacqui Small LLP, bottom, Simon Upton/© Jacqui Small LLP. Cloud Illustration on endpapers and page 12: Eva Black.

THANK YOU

This book wouldn't have been possible without all the homeowners who generously opened their doors and warmly invited me into their homes. Allowing someone into your home for a whole day is an intensely personal thing to do, and beyond the beautiful pictures I'm grateful for the new friendships forged during the making of this book. Thank you, everyone! I must also thank my dear friend Arianna and her husband Riccardo for translating between Raffaele and I while on location in Puglia, Italy. #lifesavers.

Thanks also go to the team who worked so hard with me to take Dream Decor from a one-line elevator pitch to a fully-fledged book: Jacqui for publishing; Jo for editing; Rachel for designing; Serena for illustrating and Andrew for photographing. Without your talents this book wouldn't be a patch on how it has turned out – cheers. Also thanks to my agent, Judy, for her guidance and sound advice throughout the project.

High fives to my close pals for cheerleading when mountains seemed unsurpassable; to Brooke for helping with my 'arty' signature; and to my husband, Toby, for his boundless support, energy and ability to make me laugh – I can't wait for our new adventures in New York City.

Finally, thank you to you for reading the book. I do hope it helps you create your dream decor wherever you happen to live right now. Stop by and say hi on Instagram (@brightbazaar) anytime. Until then, stay colourful!